Mind, Heart, and Soul

Mind, Heart, and Soul

Intellectuals and the
Path to Rome

Edited by Robert P. George & R. J. Snell

TAN Books
Charlotte, North Carolina

Cover design by Tarina Weese

Cover Image: The dome of Saint Peters Basilica seen through the famous keyhole at the Villa Malta. Rome, Italy, Southern Europe

Library of Congress Control Number: 2018951683

ISBN: 978-1-5051-1121-7

Published in the United States by
TAN Books
PO Box 410487
Charlotte, NC 28241
www.TANBooks.com

Printed in the United States of America

Contents

Preface

Every Catholic is a convert.

While useful, the distinction often made between "cradle Catholics" and "converts" is not quite true. After all, one is baptized a Catholic, not born as such. However brief the time between birth and baptism—perhaps mere days or hours—it is through baptism and not birth that "we are freed from sin and reborn as sons of God; we become members of Christ, are incorporated into the Church and made sharers in her mission," in the words of the *Catechism*. During those hours or days between cradle and font, the "cradle Catholic" is not yet a new creature; that is, not yet a Catholic.

Every Catholic is a convert, too, in that each suffers from a frail and weak human nature, and baptism does not abolish the inclination to sin. We are invited, thus, as the *Catechism* states, to "the struggle of *conversion* directed toward holiness and eternal life to which the Lord never ceases to call us." We convert many times, perhaps daily, as we repent, confess, and do penance for our sins, whether raised in the Catholic faith or not.

Nonetheless, many "cradle Catholics" have a tender fascination for those who have converted later in life, tellingly captured in the winsome phrase "welcome home." Home, where one is always welcome simply because one belongs.

From the perspective of the adult convert, cradle Catholics enjoy the remarkable good fortune of having always belonged, knowing they were part of the family, even if a sometimes rambunctious and squabbling one. Many converts struggled and resisted and protested on their way home, even as they longed for it, a struggle sometimes foreign to the experience of the cradle Catholic for whom the Church is part of the constant fabric of reality. One doesn't really pay much attention to the furnishings and arrangements of one's home, since it's inconspicuous, just the way it is and has always been as long as one can remember. When a guest visits and remarks on the sofa or the end table, for instance, it can serve as an almost startling reminder of what had become so familiar as to be unremarkable.

And converts seem to find it all remarkable, don't they? They're eager to learn this practice, to read that text—to familiarize themselves with all the furnishings of home—and they often want to share just how remarkable it is with everyone, even (or perhaps especially) with those who already know it well.

For many, although certainly not all, converts entering the Catholic Church as adults, whether from another Christian community, another religion, or no faith at all, the Catholic intellectual tradition was experienced as part of the struggle to come home. Some turned to the Patristics for guidance, others to the Scholastics, yet others to the mystical or spiritual authors. For some, no one period or figure stands out as much as the entire "symphony" of truth found in the Catholic traditions of music, poetry, art, theology, literature, and moral philosophy.

Often, other converts smooth the way, offering companionship on the sometimes-difficult path to Rome.

Intellectuals who've converted help other intellectuals find their way home. This was certainly true of the figures comprising what some term the "Catholic Renaissance" of the mid-nineteenth to mid-twentieth century. During that time, a great crowd of highly influential English-speaking intellectuals converted to Catholicism, including John Henry Newman, G. K. Chesterton, Christopher Dawson, Orestes Brownson, Ronald Knox, Graham Greene, Evelyn Waugh, Thomas Merton, Dorothy Day, Robert Hugh Benson, and many others. To these English-speaking figures, one could add Edith Stein, the Maritains, Paul Claudel, Léon Bloy, Charles Péguy, Gabriel Marcel, and Dietrich von Hildebrand. Of them all, one could say, citing Patrick Allitt, that "when the church began to reassert herself in the nineteenth century, it used converts as its principal advocates. . . . Many of their contemporaries regarded the ideas of a 'Catholic intellectual' as a contradiction in terms, believing that the repressive Roman church prohibited freedom of thought. The converts were eager to prove otherwise; their work in history, science, literature, and philosophy was designed to substantiate their belief that Catholicism was intellectually liberating rather than restrictive, despite the church's dogmatic style and hierarchical structure."[1]

The great wave of the Catholic Renaissance helped fuel the apologists of the last several decades, including Thomas Howard, Peter Kreeft, Karl Keating, Dwight Longenecker, and Scott Hahn, to name a few, each a convert playing a well-known role in the conversion of others. And from them there have been in just the past few years a flurry of books from a third wave of younger intellectuals writing

---

[1]   Patrick Allitt, *Catholic Converts: British and American Intellectuals Turn to Rome* (Cornell University Press, 2000), 1–3. See also Charles P. Connor, *Classic Catholic Converts* (Ignatius, 2001).

on their conversions. Each wave enriches the witness of the Church, and such conversion stories provide encouragement and signs of hope. All too frequently we're told that science makes faith irrelevant, and then we learn of an astrophysicist or a philosopher converting. We hear of the rise of the "nones," young people without any religious commitment, but then we read of a young journalist or accomplished novelist who finds in the Church a source of stability, truth, and wisdom. We're informed the Church must "update" its moral teachings to stay relevant, but then discover that a good many converts enter the Church precisely because her moral theology offers sanity, humanity, and a path to human flourishing.

In this text, a cradle Catholic (Robert P. George) and an adult convert (R. J. Snell), offer the stories of sixteen converts, each a public intellectual or leading voice in their respective fields, and each making a significant contribution to the life of the Church. To do so, we've asked an array of other intellectuals, many who are themselves converts, to conduct interviews to learn more about the journey to Rome.

While some of the intellectuals interviewed are known as converts, none have written extensively on their conversion and their stories are largely unknown. Here they speak, providing the reasons for belief that prompted these accomplished men and women to embrace the ancient Faith.

★★★

We wish to offer our gratitude to each of the contributors to this text, whether interviewer or interviewee, for their efforts and goodwill in putting the book together. We are also thankful to the publishers and staff at TAN Books, especially John Moorehouse and Conor Gallagher.

***

While this text will be published after the widely-reported Church scandals of August 2018, the interviews themselves were completed prior to those reports and do not address them in any way.

At times such as these, we might wish to learn how those interviewed grapple with such terrible events, perhaps especially if, as a new convert, their homecoming was marred by the grave and horrible actions by some within the Church.

We cannot speak for those interviewed about those matters, but we do offer their conversion stories as signs that while we do not place our trust in princes (Ps. 146: 3), we continue to trust in a God who does not abandon us and who, in the words of one Eucharistic prayer, will "never cease to gather a people to [Himself], so that from the rising of the sun to its setting a pure sacrifice may be offered to [His] name."

If converts continue to enter our Church, bruised and shattered as she is, it is because of the grace of God. It is our hope that these conversion stories remind their readers that God is faithful to save, and that Our Lord continues to suffer with and for us.

Chapter One

"Cor ad Cor Loquitur":
Cardinal Newman and
the Bishop of Lincoln

Most Reverend James D. Conley, DD, STL
Bishop of Lincoln, Nebraska

Interviewed by Robert P. George

Bishop James D. Conley was ordained a priest in 1985, serving as a parish priest in the Diocese of Wichita before earning his licentiate in Rome, where he later returned to serve as an official in the Vatican Congregation for Bishops. In 2001, Pope John Paul II named him "chaplain to his holiness" with the title of Monsignor. In 2008, Pope Benedict XVI appointed him as auxiliary bishop for the Archdiocese of Denver, with Denver Archbishop Charles J. Chaput ordaining him. Later, he would serve as apostolic administrator of the Denver Archdiocese, until Pope Benedict appointed him as the bishop of the Lincoln Diocese in Nebraska. Bishop Conley was installed as the ninth bishop of Lincoln on November 20, 2012 in the Cathedral of the Risen Christ in Lincoln.

For his episcopal motto, Bishop Conley, a convert to the Catholic faith, chose the same motto as the great nineteenth-century English convert John Henry Cardinal Newman, "*cor ad cor loquitur*," which means "heart speaks to heart."

Robert P. George holds Princeton's celebrated McCormick Chair in Jurisprudence and is the director of the James Madison Program in American Ideals and Institutions. He has served as chairman of the United States Commission on International Religious Freedom, and before that on the President's Council on Bioethics and as a presidential appointee to the United States Commission on Civil Rights. He has also served as the US member of UNESCO's World Commission on the Ethics of Scientific Knowledge and Technology. His many books include *In Defense of Natural Law; Making Men Moral; Embryo: A Defense of Human Life*; and *What is Marriage? Man and Woman: A Defense.* A graduate of Swarthmore College, he holds JD and MTS degrees from Harvard University and the degrees of D.Phil., BCL, and DCL from Oxford University.

Robert P. George: *Please tell us about your upbringing. Were you brought up in the Christian faith?*

Bishop Conley: I was brought up nominally Christian. My parents were both Christian, but for a large portion of my youth, we didn't go to church. Then for a few years we went to the Presbyterian church, only because my mother liked the preacher. But my sister and I didn't have any formal religious instruction growing up. My parents were Christian in their outlook and instilled in us Christian values, but we really didn't worship together as a family. We would go to church sometimes on Christmas and Easter. During junior high we went to Sunday school off and on.

Had you been baptized as a child?

Actually, it was kind of doubtful. In seventh grade, we had a class in which the preacher sprinkled everybody with water, but I couldn't really recall much about it. I was never given a baptismal certificate, so when I was received into the Catholic Church, I was conditionally baptized.

Had you become serious about the Christian faith before considering being received into the Catholic Church? Did you have a period of time in another Christian denomination or anything like that?

I really didn't. It wasn't until I arrived at the University of Kansas and enrolled in its great books program, the Integrated Humanities Program, that I began thinking seriously about "the permanent things," like goodness, truth, and beauty, and eternity, life, death, the problem of good and evil, justice and mercy. I hadn't really thought about those great ideas until I was eighteen years old and in college.

So it sounds from what you say as though your intellectual inquiries were quite integral to your spiritual journey?

They were. I used to say for many years that I read my way to the Catholic Church, which was true to a certain extent. The "great books" of Western civilization introduced me to the towering authors of the Western tradition. And as you know, in programs like that we read many pagan authors— the Greeks and Romans—as well as Christian authors. I learned from all of them. And my reading led me to think more and more about the big, existential questions—about God and religion and my place in the world.

Eventually I began going to church. I did some church hopping here and there. I attended the Episcopal Church for a few months, but it was a short pit stop. Finally, I found my way to the Catholic Church. As I said, it was certainly an intellectual journey for me, but as I get older I can say that it was the friendships I made during those years and the example of virtue in other people that played the biggest role in my journey of faith. Others who were on the same journey, the same quest, had a great influence on my heart and my imagination and my will. We were all reading the same books and discussing these great ideas together. We were supporting and helping each other.

Are there one or two of those friends you could speak more specifically about?

I can tell you about two people who had a tremendous influence on me and my conversion to the Catholic Church. One is my longest and closest friend. We grew up together, went to high school together, then went to the university together. We were roommates all four years in college. He's now the archbishop of Oklahoma City, Paul Coakley. He was a cradle Catholic but, like all of us, was searching during those early years of college in the 1970s. He came back full force into the Catholic Church during those years. My other roommate was a gentleman by the name of Alan Hicks. He, too, was in the IHP and also converted to Catholicism a few years before I did. Now he is teaching at my seminary here in the Diocese of Lincoln.

How wonderful.

Yes, it really is. And I should also mention our professors at the University, especially Professor John Senior who ended up being my godfather, and who has written with great illumination about education and about the restoration of Christian culture. I should also mention Dennis Quinn and Frank Nelick who were the other two professors in the program. Incidentally, last year a book was published on the life of John Senior by a monk at Clear Creek Abbey in Oklahoma who's also a former student of Professor Senior. And so we had a big reunion on the occasion of the book launch last summer. The book was published by Thomas

More Press under the title *The Restoration of Realism*. That's an appropriate title since one of the principal goals of the IHP was to bring the students back to real things—real friendships, real literature, poetry, music, art, architecture, the outdoors. The motto of the IHP was *Nascantur in Admiratione* ("let them be born in wonder").

The program, actually, played a role in the conversion of a great many students. We counted them once and discovered that there were over three hundred conversions of students involved in the program in a period of about ten years. Some converts became priests, two became bishops, one became an abbot, others entered religious orders, including monastic ones. But the majority were called to the vocation of marriage and raised families. Those children now are married and, in most cases, having children of their own. It just kind of continues, the ripple effect continues to spread.

It sounds like the Holy Spirit was working overtime!

Yeah. It was unique and, in a way, ironic because, as you know, the 1970s was a time of great cultural upheaval, of social revolution and rebellion in universities. And this was something different—they called it an "experiment in tradition." And it was happening right in the midst of one of the most secular university campuses in the country—the University of Kansas. The great books program just flourished—so much so that the university eventually shut it down because it had become too popular.

Oh my.

We called it "death by administration." But it really did flourish for about fifteen years from around 1970 to 1985.

Well, it sounds like there's quite a lesson in that for those of us who are working on the project of academic reform in higher education today.

Yes. No doubt about it. I am amazed at how many people I meet who have heard about the Integrated Humanities Program at the University of Kansas and are curious about why it was so successful.

I think we can learn from the success of serious great books programs. I'm not talking here specifically or only about religious conversions, though it is interesting that so many students in the program converted to Catholicism. I'm remarking on the way the students were willing to have their lives shaped by reading and reflection.

Yes, this is the principal reason why, here at the University of Nebraska, we started a new institute called the Newman Institute for Catholic Thought and Culture. I had the idea of creating something like what we had at the University of Kansas. Interestingly, 90 percent of all college age Catholic students are at public universities. Only 10 percent are at Catholic universities. So the vast majority of our Catholic college students are on secular campuses. My thought was to create a vigorous and robust intellectual and cultural life on campus by offering these courses and also engendering friendships—good Christian friendships founded on truth, goodness and beauty—and thus creating a real community. We launched the Institute two years ago. Dr. John Freeh, who is our founding director, is now teaching this program, and it's growing steadily.

That is marvelous. What a gift to your students. You've spoken a bit, Bishop Conley, about the role of friends and of mentors in your own intellectual-spiritual journey. Could we talk a bit about writers and thinkers, especially people from the past, who influenced you? We're telling your story, not mine, but I'll just say a word about my own experience to set up a question I'd like to ask. I was brought up in the Catholic faith and was never alienated from it. I've always been a practicing Catholic. But if I look back at the moments that really deepened and reinforced my faith, among the handful I would point to was my encounter with a non-Catholic—indeed a pagan—a non-Christian author, and that was Plato—especially his dialogue Gorgias. *I have a sense that my experience is not unique among Catholics and among Catholic converts. It might be different with Christians of other traditions, but for Catholics the enrichment of the Faith is often occasioned by the encounter with great thinkers of all types, including classical philosophers. When you think back to the writers and thinkers who influenced you from the past, who are the ones that immediately come to mind? Who are the ones who seem to have had the greatest impact on your development?*

Okay, very good question. I resonate very strongly with your experience. It was, again, the authors that we read in that two-year freshman/sophomore great books program who introduced me to the great ideas of Western civilization. We, too, read the *Dialogues* of Plato, but we also read the *Iliad* and the *Odyssey* by Homer, as well as Virgil's *Aeneid* and many other classic works, both pagan and Christian. These works caused me to think of ideas such as truth, goodness, and beauty for the first time in my life. They opened up for me a whole new world of intellectual ideas. Two authors in particular had a profound impact on me at that time in my life: Saint Augustine and Blessed John Henry Newman. When I read St. Augustine's *Confessions*, it had a tremendous impact on me. But Newman had perhaps even a greater and more enduring impact on my life.

In fact, I took Newman's own motto as a cardinal, *cor ad cor loquitur* ("heart speaks to heart"), as my own episcopal motto. His journey into the Catholic Church from Anglicanism was something that completely captivated my own imagination and intellect. In my sophomore year, we read selections from Newman's *Idea of a University* in the IHP. This was when I first encountered Newman. But it wasn't until my junior year in a British authors survey course when I had to write a paper on Newman, as an example of a nineteenth-century English prose writer, that I fell in love with him. The more I read of Newman, the more I wanted to read. And that hasn't stopped since. Not unlike two other great converts, St. Paul and St. Augustine, to read Newman is to know Newman. It is hard to separate his writings from his life. Newman is my go-to person for just about everything. He has certainly been the biggest influence on my intellectual life. On top of that, I think he's a saint, and I believe that one day he will be proclaimed a doctor of the church.

Of course, there were great authors who followed Newman, including some who were part of the Oxford movement. And then there were people like Gerard Manley Hopkins, G. K. Chesterton, Hilaire Belloc, J. R. R. Tolkien, Graham Greene, Evelyn Waugh, and Ronald Knox, the so-called Catholic literary revival in England.

Was Newman's Essay in Aid of a Grammar of Assent *an important work for you?*

It was! Funny you should mention that, because that's one of his least known and most difficult philosophical works.

I ask about it only because it was an important one for me.

Most people don't point to that book because it is not an easy read. Alan Hicks, one of my former roommates who is now teaching at my seminary, and I read it aloud together. He was a philosophy major, and I was an English major. I was having difficulty understanding Newman's argument and of course he, being deeply immersed in philosophy, was catching on to the argument a bit more easily. So we read through it together, and that was very helpful. I particularly remember Newman's distinction between "notional assent" and "real assent" to the truth; how our apprehension of knowledge must go beyond the head (notional) to the heart (real); we must make it our own.

When I myself was reading Newman's Grammar of Assent, *I was at the same time reading Bernard Lonergan's magnum opus* Insight: A Study of Human Understanding.

Lonergan was very popular in seminaries in the 1970s. I was in the seminary in the '80s and by then his work wasn't as popular, though it certainly hadn't fallen out of favor. I read a bit of his writing, but not a lot.

Some of our evangelical Protestant friends—certainly not all, but some—worry that we Catholics tend to over-intellectualize things, that our faith is perhaps a bit too rationalist. What's your reaction to that concern?

That's another good question. Of course, faith and reason really are complementary. There is no conflict between them. And I think that one of the crises of today is a crisis of reason. Some people—some secular people—seem to think we need to jettison reason. They embrace subjectivism or relativism, especially when it comes to moral questions. They give up on the idea that reason is a truth-attaining faculty.

Do you have in mind "post modernism," "deconstruction," those approaches or ideologies?

Exactly. Catholicism teaches a high view of reason. Reason is not the enemy of faith. Quite the contrary. As I said, reason and faith are complementary. They can and do work together. God doesn't contradict reason. God gave us minds—intellects—for the sake of pursuing the knowledge of truth. When reason is denied its proper role, we easily go astray. The heart is important, but if it's all from the heart, and reason does not inform our faith, we are vulnerable.

Now, can we over-intellectualize the faith? Yes, that's possible. We can fall into the error of rationalism. And I think that's a criticism that Catholics sometimes receive, and not always unjustly. You know, I have a great appreciation for the Evangelical Protestant emphasis on the need for all of us to have a personal relationship with Jesus. It's true and important.

I think we're learning that from our evangelical friends. It's something that the Catholic Church always taught, but something that I think Catholics didn't appreciate enough.

That's a very good point. It's true. At first, many Catholics were somewhat averse to that. It made them a bit uncomfortable. It was awkward for us to talk in those "Protestant-sounding" terms. But we have come more deeply to understand that our faith must convict every part of the soul (affective as well as intellective) and body. The whole person enters into a relationship with Jesus. And this friendship with the Lord is cultivated by prayer and nurtured in witness.

Newman's first conversion was to a particular doctrinal creed when he was a mere youth of sixteen. He came to realize that the human mind can come to understand that there is a God, and that we can come to know God through our intellect. We are thinking beings, rational creatures. We can know truths about the natural world, the human and social world, even the supernatural world.

But faith concerns the mind and the heart. Faith commands the whole person. Evangelicals are right to emphasize the need for each of us to be a friend of Jesus and to understand what that means and to live that friendship through our prayers, through our charity, through our relationships or friendships with others. And through our intellects as well. This is what I think Newman meant when he wrote about going from the notional to the real in the apprehension of faith. He once famously said, no one will die for a conclusion, but many have given their life for a person.

Let me ask a couple of questions that have to do with the work you do now and your experience coming to that work as a convert to the Catholic faith. The first is general. How do you think your being a convert affects your work as a bishop?

Well, as a convert, you're always a convert. It's almost part of my identity. I became a Catholic over forty years ago, but I'm still a convert. People know that I'm a convert because I talk about my conversion a lot; people know my story. I'm one of only three bishops in the United States who are converts to the Catholic faith. And I must say that it's very helpful in preaching and teaching because people seem to kind of perk up and listen when I speak about my conversion. I don't know why that is, but it's something that I find to be very effective in my preaching and teaching. If I'm speaking to an audience of both Catholics and non-Catholics, the non-Catholics tend to listen particularly attentively because of the fact that I was myself a non-Catholic who found his way to the Catholic faith. But the Catholics also find it fascinating that there would be someone who was not born into Catholic faith—who came to it later in life—who is now a bishop. Sometimes you hear people say, "Catholic converts are the best Catholics." Why? I don't think that's true. But what is true is that converts seem to maintain a freshness about the Faith; a kind of newness about the Faith.

You know, I converted over forty years ago. And yet I still look at the Catholic faith as something new to me. It's something that I'm still learning, I'm still a novice at it, you know? And even though now I'm a bishop, I am still excited about my conversion. And that's one thing I think is generally true with all converts.

I'm sure you're right about that. Now, I guess that, as a technical matter, all Christians are converts to the Christian faith. None of us is literally born into it. We were baptized into Christ's death and resurrection. But I think we all know what we mean when we're talking about converts, as we are in this conversation.

We're all on a journey. Some of us started on it a bit earlier, some later.

Let me ask my second question about how your experience as a convert has shaped your episcopal work and witness. We live in the post-Vatican II era in which ecumenism and interreligious cooperation are important parts of the work of the Church. We've got the division between the East and the West that goes back now ten or eleven centuries, and we're so desperate to heal. It has been a great hope of recent popes, especially Pope St. John Paul II and Pope Benedict XVI, that we would finally heal it. And there's the division within the West between Protestants and Catholics. Then there's the special relationship (and a tragic, and fraught history) that Catholics and all Christians have with the Jewish people. How has your experiences as a convert shaped your work in respect of ecumenism and interreligious relations?

Well, I feel comfortable in a mixed crowd of Catholics and non-Catholics, Christians and non-Christians. I have great respect for people of all faiths. As I mentioned, I did some church hopping before my conversion to the Catholic Church and made some "pit stops" in different Christian denominations. I believe very strongly in what the Church teaches about the need to honor all that is true and good and beautiful in the non-Christian traditions. But I am a convinced Catholic Christian that all salvation comes through Jesus Christ and his one, holy, catholic and apostolic Church, outside of which there is no salvation. I believe the Catholic Church is the true Church established by Christ himself. So I want others to enter the Church. Of course, I don't harangue people or anything like that. No true or effective evangelist does that. I respect people's own faith traditions and how they came to God; I listen to what they have to say; I try to understand where they're coming from and why they believe what they believe. But deep down inside, you know, my prayer is always, "You should become Catholic." I want you part of the one true body of Christ. I have a brother-in-law who's Jewish, and my sister who's still searching. I love them both dearly. My mother and father were received into the Catholic Church in 1991. I had the privilege of baptizing and confirming them and giving them their First Holy Communion. My father died in 2006 in the arms of Holy Mother Church and my mother just turned ninety last month.

What a joy that must have been for you . . . and them!

Yes, it happened after I was about six years a priest. They converted, and my only niece converted in 2015. But there are many people who are very close to me who are not Catholic, and who may never become Catholic. So, kind of living in that tension is a bit awkward. But at the same time, I don't let that stop me from having good, loving relationships with them. There was a time when I was younger and sometimes found myself sticking my foot in my mouth in my zeal to convert the world. I sometimes got into unproductive arguments and perhaps turned people off. In the zeal of conversion, you don't always say the right thing.

But even now I want people to come to Christ and to the Church. That doesn't mean I don't respect their traditions. I do. And I accept the fact that they may never become Catholic. I can live with that. But I don't want to fall into the heresy which says, "Well, you know, everybody is going to heaven, so it doesn't really matter what one believes." A faithful Catholic cannot endorse religious relativism or indifferentism.

When one thinks about this, it's something that we Catholics share with serious believers of other faiths, certainly with many of the great historical religious traditions. If they believe, which they must, that the teachings of their faith are true, presumably they believe that those who reject those teachings or hold beliefs that are inconsistent with them are in error on those points. And they surely further believe that those who are in error would be better off believing what's true. Indeed, how could someone not wish for others to enter into the fullness of truth? So it doesn't sound to me as though what we are talking about here is uniquely a Catholic issue. Consider Islam. Our Muslim friends who are serious about their faith have the same issue. So do our Jewish friends, although Judaism in the modern period is not an evangelizing or missionizing religion.

I agree.

So if one believes that Jesus is a great man, and perhaps even a prophet, but not the Son of God, you don't want—or shouldn't want—people to remain in error about that. Not if you think truth is important. But at the same time, you don't want to get into big, fruitless arguments with people who believe that Jesus is the Son of God. You respect their faith, you respect that they have thought about the question and landed where they landed, perhaps erroneously but nevertheless sincerely. And you do try to work together where you do share convictions, principles, and values.

Yes. Absolutely. I agree. I think that's a good way to put it.

May I ask you a bit about the pontificate of Pope St. John Paul II? You were basically formed as a priest in that pontificate. Do you have reflections on Pope St. John Paul II himself?

I do. In fact, I can trace the spark of my vocation to an encounter with him on October 4, 1979, during his very first visit to the United States. One of the stops on that historic visit was in Des Moines, Iowa. It was the Feast of Saint Francis, and I was there with a bunch of college friends. I had finished my studies at the University of Kansas and had only been a Catholic for a few years. I didn't really know where I was headed or what I was going to do with my life. I was dating a girl at the time and we all went up to see this new pope. At the end of the outdoor Mass, the Holy Father made this plea to young men, as he always did, inviting them to consider the priesthood. From that day forward, I started thinking seriously about a vocation to the priesthood. And within three months, I was in the seminary.

Suffice it to say, John Paul II had a tremendous impact on my life. Throughout my seminary years and my entire priesthood, right up until his death, he continued profoundly to influence me. I was called to Rome to work in the Vatican Congregation for Bishops in 1996 and served in that position for ten years. Nine of those years were during his pontificate. My last year in Rome was under the pontificate of Pope Benedict XVI.

Did you know him personally?

I met him on several occasions, but I did not know him well. He might have recognized my face, but probably not remembered my name or exactly in what office I served.

Did you, or do you, know Pope Benedict XVI?

Well, in 2008 Pope Benedict named me to serve as auxiliary bishop in Denver. And then he appointed me bishop of Lincoln in 2012. But even before that, I was heavily influenced by his work as a theologian and as the Prefect of the Congregation for the Doctrine of the Faith. I did have opportunities to get to know him when he was serving in that position. We spent a lot of time together in collaborative meetings between the Congregation for Bishops, where I was on the staff, and the Congregation for the Doctrine of the Faith. I also had friends who worked on the staff at the CDF, and so we would have occasions, both formal and informal, to spend time with him. His theological writings have also meant a great deal to me and have helped to shape my ministry as a priest and now as a bishop.

Could we talk a bit, Bishop Conley, about the challenges facing the Church today? Obviously, there are profound divisions within the Church. There's no point I think in any Catholic trying to hide that fact. Indeed, there are divisions among bishops. There are divisions over some very fundamental issues, especially moral issues, such as those pertaining to marriage. Are we in trouble?

Well, we're in trouble as a culture and as a civilization, to be sure. With regard to the institution of marriage and our understanding of human sexuality and moral theology, the moral life, yes, we're in big trouble. As a Church, the situation is somewhat complicated. I have a licentiate in moral theology from a Pontifical University and I've taught moral theology at the college level, so I follow these issues very closely. And I also Chair the Subcommittee for the Promotion and Defense of Marriage for the United States Conference of the Catholic Bishops. So I'm immersed in these issues. With the pontificate of Pope Francis, there have been questions raised about what we had up to this point accepted as settled Catholic moral teaching on marriage and human sexuality. Now, I think we should and do still uphold that teaching. I certainly do. And I think Pope Francis still does as well. I love his writings on marriage and on human sexuality, as well as things he has written on culture of life issues, human ecology and the environment, immigration, and human dignity. He's been a great light and a great leader in those areas.

When it comes to the understanding of marriage and human sexuality, there seem to be some voices within the Church, some at a very high level, that are calling into question some fundamental truths about the human person. These truths have long been taught by the Church and were strongly reaffirmed by Pope John Paul and Pope Benedict. Questions concerning the nature and function of conscience, sin and the moral act, intrinsic evil, and the natural law. You ask: "Is the Church in trouble?" Well, you know, I think there are some voices that are very disturbing. And some of them are very important voices—theologians and even bishops, archbishops, and cardinals. Still, I am not shaken. Maybe it's because I'm a convert and have confidence in the Holy Spirit. I always go back to "the hermeneutic of continuity" as Pope Benedict would call it.

Even though there are some troubling trends and deepening divisions within the Church, I have confidence that the Holy Spirit will eventually sort it all out and not let the Church go off the rails. I suspect that within the next five years we are going to confront a lot of the things that are causing uncertainty and division.

But, you know, I think it's been good that we have been looking at these things. This year is the fiftieth anniversary of *Humanae Vitae*, arguably the most important papal encyclical in the last one hundred years. There are going to be some very important conferences coming up, particularly the one at Catholic University of America in April of this year. They're going to deal head-on with these questions. I know that there have been theologians who have called into question some fundamental elements of *Humanae Vitae*, like the concept of intrinsically evil acts, and other very fundamental truths. But I don't think they are going to win the day. I just think that basic moral truths of this sort are so deeply embedded in our tradition that they will not be dislodged, no matter what a cardinal might say, or even what the pope might say. I mean, even the highest authority in the Church cannot change teachings that are infallibly proposed by the ordinary magisterium of the Church. And what we're talking about here are teachings that are infallibly proposed—consistently, persistently, and insistently over the decades—by the ordinary universal magisterium.

That's a sometimes-overlooked truth, but a truth nonetheless.

One of the things that Pope Francis has brought to us in a beautiful way is the idea of accompaniment and of reaching out to those who are on the margins, the people who are living in situations that are either irregular by way of marriage or are struggling with gender identity, those kinds of things. He rightly insists that it cannot be the pastoral practice of the Church to turn our faces away from those people. We have to reach out and understand why they're struggling, what they're going through. That's good and we must continue to do that. I try to do that.

Our subcommittee published an "open letter" shortly before Christmas called "Created Male and Female." It was signed by four Catholic bishops but also by other Christian leaders and leaders of other faiths. It addressed gender ideology and transgenderism. It does not condemn people, and it tries to understand where people who embrace and promote gender ideology are coming from. But we cannot forfeit what we know to be true about the human person, which is that God made us male and female and we can't change that.

Do you share the view that a large part of the future of the Church, and that much of the future leadership of the Church, will be coming from Africa and other places that have been thought of historically in the Church, at least for many centuries, as "mission fields"?

Yes, I do. And perhaps it's going to come in a way we don't anticipate. There are large bodies of Catholic Christians in South America and Africa. We are seeing a great many conversions to the Catholic faith, especially in Africa. They're just bound to have an influence on the universal Church. And that's a good thing. Their faith is real and vibrant. And they are giving us priests, and bishops, and cardinals—maybe soon a pope.

African Catholics have a freshness and a kind of a robust faith that is invigorating for the Church. We need that. The Church in Western countries, particularly in Western Europe is just not growing, it is actually shrinking at an alarmingly accelerating rate. Just do the math, the majority of Catholics are going to be coming from the developing world—and that means the majority of priests, majority of bishops, the majority of cardinals, and maybe popes in the future.

Have you had occasions to work closely, perhaps during your time at the Vatican, with some of the African bishops?

My first Prefect, or boss, when I came to Rome as an official in the Congregation for Bishops was Cardinal Bernardin Gantin, who was from Benin, Africa. He was a very impressive man and had a very interesting background. He was a prince of an African tribe and a convert to the Catholic faith. He had a tremendous influence on me. My first three years in Rome were under him. He was a physically impressive man, too, large, standing about 6'4". I remember him very well and think of him often. Then there was Cardinal Lucas Moreira Neves—a Brazilian who was the Prefect following Cardinal Gantin. And then there is Cardinal Robert Sarah—another great African convert to the Faith. I got to know him through one of our Lincoln priests who currently serves under Cardinal Sarah in the Congregation for Divine Worship and Discipline of Sacraments.

You know, living in Rome, it's such an international place. I lived there for ten years, so I met prelates from everywhere. Cardinal Arinze, for example, another great African. Cardinal Jorge Maria Mejia, from Argentina, was a former Secretary of the Congregation for Bishops and was a like a second father to me when I first moved to Rome in 1996. I was very impressed with the prelates I met, not least those from the developing world.

I'd like to shift to a topic that's of special importance to me as a professor of philosophy of law and moral and political philosophy. Let me provide a little preface to the question. I myself believe and have argued that many principles we think of as Enlightenment principles are those we as Catholic Christians can and should embrace. Often these are principles that, in truth, are anchored in pre-Enlightenment traditions, including in some aspects of medieval thought. An example is the principle of religious freedom.

As you know, the idea of religious liberty struck some eighteenth- and nineteenth-century Catholic leaders, notably including popes, as a possibly dangerous one because they associated it with some aspects of French Revolutionary ideology. Here I think the experience of the United States and of Catholicism in the United States and the work of people like John Courtney Murray were helpful in enabling us to see that it is possible to fashion and affirm a doctrine of religious liberty that does not embrace religious relativism or indifferentism or involve hostility to religion and to the Church.

Today, however, there are thinkers, some of them good thinkers, good Catholic thinkers, who believe that the Church perhaps was wrong to embrace the "Enlightenment principle" of religious freedom. Or they think that the Church went too far in endorsing a wide, robust conception of religious freedom. Or they counsel us to read Dignitatis Humanae *narrowly. And sometimes they express skepticism about democracy or a broad conception of rights of democratic participation, such as the conception stressed by Pope John Paul II. Some critics of this sort call themselves (or are called by their own critics) "Catholic integralists." They stand opposed to the teaching of someone who was very influential in the development of my own thinking and was a dear friend; namely, Father Richard John Neuhaus. Fr. Neuhaus affirmed what he believed, and I myself believe, are the great and true principles of the Declaration of Independence and of the Constitution of the United States. Neuhaus didn't see those principles as alien to Christian faith generally, or Catholic faith in particular, but rather as principles that Catholics and other Christians can and should uphold. What's your own reflection on the question of "integralism" and religious freedom and other so-called Enlightenment principles?*

You've asked another important question. And again, I go back to Newman. Newman was really a child of the Enlightenment and it's not difficult to perceive its influence on his thought. He in turn influenced the broader Church. In fact, he is sometimes referred to as a kind of "silent father" of the Second Vatican Council. He helped to sort the good from the bad in the ideas of Enlightenment thinkers, and through his writings, he helped the Church see what it should embrace as healthy and what it should reject as incompatible with the Gospel and the tradition of the Church.

On the question of democracy and how it relates to Christianity in general, I find myself always going back to the French political philosopher Alexis de Tocqueville. A democracy is only as good as the people whom the citizens elect to govern. In a true democracy, the people, through their elected leaders, have a real role in governing themselves. Especially as an American I believe that, just as I believe that religious freedom and freedom of speech are fundamental to the dignity of the human person.

But, you know, as we decline as a culture, and as we decline as people, morally and spiritually; as more and more people check that box "none" when it comes to faith; as more and more people lose or fail to acquire the virtues taught and nurtured by religion, and specifically the Judeo-Christian tradition, the quality of our democracy itself declines. Our founding fathers themselves understood that the quality of republican government depended on more than merely the formal structures of the Constitution. They knew that virtue was required of the electorate, and that religion is a primary teacher of virtue. Now, some of the founding fathers had rather strange religious beliefs. Not all were truly Christians. Some were deists or whatever. But they still embraced common understanding of Christian moral principles, those of the Ten Commandments, for example; and these principles informed their ideas about human dignity, marriage and the family, the common good, and the role of government. They did not opt for theocracy. But neither did they banish religion from the public square. Quite the contrary, they welcomed conversation and debate about justice and the common good; about religion, morality, and the good life, or what they called the "pursuit of happiness."

So you do not favor trying to return to a pre-modern political order?

We can't go back to that and nor should we want to return to the past. In the pre-modern period itself, monarchical rule only worked in the rare circumstances in which you had kings who were also saints. We need limits on power because rulers of any type—monarchical, aristocratic, democratic—cannot be counted on to be saints. As Christians, we know that original sin plays into this. It's great when you have a King Louis IX in France who was a saint. He won't abuse or misuse his power. But then what happens when he dies and the next one who comes along is not so virtuous and holy? The risk of tyranny becomes very real, and there are no democratic safeguards against it. You can't vote the tyrant out. Still, we need to remember in praising democracy that everything depends on the virtue, or lack thereof, in the people. And we are all fallible—Catholic Christians included.

You'll recall that Newman refers to conscience as "the primordial Vicar of Christ." It seems to me that there are two ways of understanding that idea. They take us in radically opposed directions. One way—a way Newman certainly did not have in mind— views conscience as a subjective power to determine right or wrong for oneself. It boils down to a power, posed as a right, to manufacture one's own moral universe—one in which the person creates moral truth or moral norms rather than discovering or discerning them.

The other way of understanding the idea is what I'm confident Newman had in mind. It presupposes that we are obligated to form our consciences correctly. As Catholics, that means forming our consciences in light of the teaching of the magisterium of the Church. So, yes, we are obligated to follow our consciences. But we must remember, as Newman said in his famous letter to the Duke of Norfolk, that "conscience is a stern monitor." It's not in the business of writing permission slips to authorize conduct that the magisterium of the Church teaches us is immoral. It is not what Newman contrasted it with, the corrupt idea of "conscience as self-will"—an idea that Newman said had already become dominant, especially in intellectual circles and among elites, in his own time.

Yes, I would agree with you 100 percent. I think that conscience is a key, in a certain sense, to everything we have been discussing. We have to get back to an understanding that conscience doesn't mean that I can do whatever I like or whatever I can persuade myself is acceptable or justified "for me," or "for a person in my circumstances." In a hyper-individualistic world, that puts the self at the center of everything, this is how a large segment of our society views the role of human conscience. We have a prior and primary obligation to form our consciences in line with what is true and good and beautiful. So again, it gets back to truth. What is true? We have to resist the temptation to fall into a form of relativism, one that justifies moral wrongdoing in the very name of conscience. That leads quickly to dictatorship, to the rule of power. And it disarms moral witness by removing the perspective of any kind of objective truth or objective morality, and defining wrongdoing as anything that seems unfair, or intolerant or judgmental, by those who hold power and positions of authority in society.

That's a very good point. I suppose it is what Pope-emeritus Benedict has in mind in warning of a "dictatorship of relativism."

I'm sure it is. And, you know, the more and more I think about it, the more clearly I see that he was right. I didn't quite understand fully what he meant when he first started to speak about a "dictatorship of relativism" just before he was elected pope. But as time has gone on, I see that his teaching on this is prophetic. Relativism will not tolerate a kind of "live and let live" libertarianism that some of its exponents promise. That will never be enough. What will happen—what is happening—instead is that those who believe very strongly in things that are contrary to natural law, will try to force us to believe—or force us to act as if we believed—what they believe. This new kind of relativism no longer accepts its earlier incarnation of the 1960s. The kind of relativism which engendered once familiar slogans such as, "live and let live," "to each his own," "who's to say," "if it feels good, do it." Those days are gone. The new relativists seek and wield power to force conformity with their ideology. That's the new "dictatorship."

Newman at one point said that he wasn't too keen on bringing religion into after-dinner toasts. You know, but (he went on to say) "if we must do that, then, yes, I will toast the Pope, but I will toast conscience first." Toasting conscience even ahead of the pope. That's very remarkable, don't you think?

Right. And it's very interesting on so many different levels. Of course, we have to remember once again that by "conscience" Newman means that "stern monitor." He does not mean the right to defy moral truth or make it up for oneself. An uninformed or incorrectly informed conscience is worse than useless. But let's consider what the faithful Catholic would be bound by conscience to do if, God forbid, his or her properly formed conscience were to come into conflict with something a pope says. It could be Pope Francis or any pope. Let's say a pope were to say something that contradicts or is logically inconsistent with the firm and constant teaching of the Church on a matter of faith or morals. This is rare in the long history of the Church, thank God, but it has happened. Clearly the obligation of a faithful Catholic is to honor the faith of the Church, what Newman would call the *sensus fidelium,* even above what a pope happened mistakenly to say. Popes are not dictators, nor do they govern by fiat. They are servants of the Church. One of the most ancient esteemed titles for the office of the papacy is the "Servant of the Servants of

God." The faith of the Church does not lie in a pope. Even the pope cannot overturn what has been infallibly taught, whether by the papal magisterium itself or by an ecumenical council or by the ordinary universal magisterium. The faith of the Church lies in the Church herself, as the mystical body of Christ on earth—the Christian faithful along with the bishops in union with the pope.

But if for whatever reason there's not union there, then we need to go with the *sensus fidelium*—the belief of the Church through the ages, yesterday, today, and forever. Now, the *sensus fidelium* is not to be confused with mere public opinion, or "whatever most people today think," or anything of the kind. If most people today in the West have fallen into the belief that contraception is good or acceptable, that doesn't change the Church's firm, constant, and true teaching to the contrary. When the pope reaffirms the settled teaching of Church, as soon-to-be-canonized Pope Paul VI did fifty years ago in 1968 with his encyclical *Humanae Vitae*, he was upholding and proclaiming the *sensus fidelium*.

Robby, I believe that Newman can help us with these issues today. Newman had a very healthy respect, obedience, and admiration for the papacy, but at the same time he knew that not every utterance that came out of a pope's mouth is necessarily authentic Christian doctrine. For this, he fell out of favor with many powerful figures in the Church in his day, particularly in years leading up to the First Vatican Council. It is most likely the reason he was never named a bishop. But Newman can remind us where our true faith and trust in the Church is found, and he can teach us something about how we should understand the office of Peter, especially in the present pontificate.

Chapter Two

From Utopian Community to the International Theological Commission

Sister Prudence Allen, RSM

Interviewed by Emily Sullivan

Sister Mary Prudence Allen, RSM, is a philosopher and member of the Religious Sisters of Mercy of Alma, Michigan. She received her PhD in philosophy from Claremont Graduate School of California in 1967 and then taught philosophy at Concordia University for the next thirty years. Her first major publication focusing on the philosophical concept of woman in Ancient and Medieval philosophy, *The Concept of Woman: The Aristotelian Revolution (750 BC-1250 AD)*, was published in 1985.

After Concordia, Sister Prudence taught for fifteen years at St. John Vianney Theological Seminary in Denver where she served as chair of the Philosophy Department. In 2012, the second volume of *The Concept of Woman: The Early Humanist Revolution (1250-1500)* was released.

In 2013 Sister Prudence went to Lancaster, England as part of a new Mercy foundation. In 2014, Pope Francis included Sister Prudence among the thirty theologians and philosophers he named to the International Theological Commission. In 2015, she returned to the United States. Her final volume, focusing on modern and contemporary theories about woman, was published in 2017 as *The Concept of Woman: Search for Communion of Persons (1500-2015), Volume III*.

She is presently an independent scholar lecturing and publishing and has just been assigned to help open a new convent for the Sisters of Mercy in Toledo, Ohio.

Emily Sullivan is a graduate of the great books program of Thomas Aquinas College, California. She has taught high school philosophy and theology, worked as the Northeast Program Manager for Endow and currently works for the Thomistic Institute based at the Dominican House of Studies, Washington, DC. She has spoken at Notre Dame, Princeton, and a variety of women's retreats and conferences on the thought of Sts. Thomas Aquinas, Edith Stein, and John Paul II. She and her husband have three little girls and reside in the Archdiocese of Philadelphia where Emily serves on Archbishop Chaput's Pastoral Council.

Emily Sullivan: *In the beginning of his encyclical* Fides et Ratio, *St. John Paul II writes, "God has placed in the human heart a desire to know the truth—in a word, to know himself—so that, by knowing and loving God, men and women may also come to the fullness of truth about themselves."*

For anyone serving the Church as a philosopher, this quote is bound to resonate, but does it relate to your conversion story as well? In your case, what came first: a recognition that you had an unusual hunger for the truth or was that desire already rooted in a knowledge of him who is the Truth?

Sister Prudence Allen: To answer this question, I need to describe my religious background. I was born in 1940 in Oneida, New York where some descendants of the utopian Oneida Community (1848–1881) lived in the Mansion House and in homes nearby. Both of my father's parents were born as stirpiculture children while the Oneida Community was still active. My mother was a southern Baptist from Kentucky. Because the Oneida Community was a fundamentalist Protestant Utopian community which believed that Christ had returned in AD 70, they thought that the goal of life was to live in the spirit of Christian perfection. My father was not baptized until shortly before his death. My mother, who descended from a line of ministers and Christian Cherokees, had a deep Christian faith.

Even so, we (three of my sisters and myself) were baptized together at the Episcopal Church in 1949. It was a big celebration where we were sponsored by three godparents each. We were then told by my mother that we could choose to go to whichever church we wanted to be confirmed in. Two of my sisters stayed Episcopalian, one became a Quaker, and I chose the Methodist/Congregational Church because of its very dynamic youth program. I loved going to youth camp in the summer and singing in the choir, especially the four-part hymns that are so fundamental to Methodism. It was the music that first awakened in me a sense of the sacred. During the summers I also felt the presence of God in the beauty of nature at Girl Scout camp and at our summer camp in the Adirondack mountains. I also loved to read and was surrounded by good literature both at home and at the Mansion House Library.

At sixteen I attended Northfield School for Girls in northern Massachusetts founded by Dwight L. Moody; here love for sacred music opened my heart wide to faith in God. We attended chapel every day. I noted in my diary that I loved especially particular sermons. We studied the Bible regularly and I began to get restless at the literal interpretations of all passages. In Bible class I remember arguing with the teacher about how the same passages could be interpreted analogically.

At the University of Rochester, I chose to be part of the Chapel Choir, but was beginning to become bored with this even though I kept attending. Slowly I was beginning to lose my faith, as I took courses in philosophy and pursued my major in mathematics. In my third year I chose to study in the Junior year abroad option at the University of Edinburgh. There I became very interested in David Hume's philosophy and switched my major to philosophy, a field I loved from the start.

At the same time, when I traveled with friends, I was struck by the great beauty of the Cathedral of Notre Dame in Paris, and later, on Christmas day, was taken by the haunting sound of Gregorian chant at the Benedictine Abbey of the Valley of the Fallen in Spain. These were the first Catholic churches I had ever visited. For about three years I completely lost my faith and argued against the faith with other students.

In graduate school at Claremont, I rediscovered my faith through friends who had been influenced by a Benedictine monastery in the Mojave Desert where several of the monks had been living in China and teaching at a seminary there. I had never met such intelligent men with faith, and this awakened my curiosity about how they could be both intelligent and Catholic. It took some time, but one of my friends was insistent that I read the Gospel of St. John and an article by Maritain, "Who is my neighbor?" I remember going to the parish church in Claremont and sitting in front of the tabernacle with a rough prayer: "Jesus, if you are in there, I want to know. I do not want to miss out!"

On the Third Sunday of Advent in 1964, I was received into the Roman Catholic Church with a conditional baptism at St. Andrew's Monastery, and my professors and friends from Claremont Graduate School were there. In late spring I was confirmed in the very church where I had sat in front of the tabernacle asking my rough question. I have never looked back or regretted this decision in any way.

Sometimes in conversion stories, people tend to bifurcate the human person, setting up a "head vs. heart" narrative, as if one's conversion was entirely a subjective experience rooted in the emotions and this kind of account makes up a "personal testimony." But many great Catholic academics—I'm thinking here of St. Augustine, St. Edith Stein, Bl. John Henry Newman—seem to have real watershed moments in their conversion story because of their reading or through study. For Augustine, it was encountering St. Paul in that famous "Tolle lege" moment. For Edith Stein, it was staying up all night with the biography of Teresa of Avila and, when the sun rose, she went in search of a priest. For Newman, it was the study of the Church Fathers in preparation for a book he was writing on the Arian heresy. Were books and your life of study a vital part of your conversion story, and if so, can you tell us about that?

For me, my conversion was of the whole person from beginning to end. I never experienced the head vs. heart dichotomy. In a way, it was a lot like singing, or mountain climbing, or swimming when the whole person is engaged in the activity of exploring or learning or enjoying the struggle. I wanted to learn as much as I could about the Faith. One of the challenges is that Vatican II was going on at the time of my conversion. We knew that something major was happening, but not exactly what. To add to that I was given the Dutch Catechism as the document to use to prepare. It was a very loose time. I think that I most loved the Gloria and the Creeds and kept repeating phrases from these prayers. I loved the Mass and the books we used at that time of the old form (now called the extraordinary form). The priest spoke Latin and we read the red print of the English translation. But the Latin words just kept sounding in my ears "*Hostiam puram, hostiam sanctum, hostiam immaculatam," "Mea Culpa, Mea Culpa, Mea Maxima Culpa,"* et cetera.

Except for prayerfully reading the St. Andrew's Missal and Scripture, I wouldn't say particular books influenced my conversion. However, immediately after I entered the Catholic Church, I began to devour books on the spiritual life. In particular, St. Teresa of Avila, St. John of the Cross, and St. Bernard of Clairvaux were very important to me. I usually immersed myself into one author at a time and read everything I could find that he or she had written. After I moved to Montreal and entered into spiritual direction, I read Fr. Reginald Garrigou-Lagrange and Fr. Adolphe Tanquerey for a more analytic approach to the stages of the spiritual interior life.

In the midst of this conversion, were there stumbling blocks for you? How did your family respond to your intention to enter the Church? Were there doctrinal issues that you really struggled with? How did these situations resolve?

The first stumbling block was a question in my mind about whether my awakening to Jesus Christ in graduate school was an invitation to return to my previous Protestant faith or to move toward the Catholic faith. So I decided to ask one of my professors at Claremont, who was a faithful Protestant, to meet with me about the Protestant faith (he was Presbyterian) at the same time as I was reading the *Catechism of the Catholic Faith*. We met several times, but the turning point included two things. First, he gave me a history of the Catholic faith which actually made me think that it was a miracle that it survived through many corrupt times. Second, he shared with me that in his view to be part of a church that was smaller and purer was better than to be part of a church that was bigger and included all kinds of unfaithful people. I found myself thinking that I would rather be part of a universal church open to everyone. Perhaps I was rejecting my utopian background here, but the clarification helped me to make my decision to go forward in my preparation for entry into the Catholic Church. This kind man then came to my entrance at St. Andrew's Monastery in the high Mojave Desert.

My parents were not happy about my decision to become Roman Catholic. In fact, my father told me that this was the one faith that he was prejudiced against. But they did not try to stop me, as I was twenty-four by then. Eventually, my father decided to be baptized in the Church, and he and my mother were married. They attended my final vows ceremony in the Religious Sisters of Mercy in Alma, Michigan, and by the end of their lives, they loved the Religious Sisters of Mercy so much that my father even said the only person he wanted to speak with when he was dying was our mother general.

In my early years as a Catholic, I struggled with the doctrinal issues around *Humanae Vitae* (Pope Paul VI's 1968 defense of the Church's prohibition against artificial contraception). I was very ignorant about the truths contained in the document. Only later in my life, when I studied the issues more thoroughly, did I come to realize the great depth of the teaching of the Church in this area. It was really through the Religious Sisters of Mercy, many of whom work in the health care area as physicians, nurses, trained in especially helping couples conceive through NaPro Technology and other similar natural methods, that I came to appreciate the great wisdom of *Humanae Vitae.*

Decades after you entered the Church, you now not only live as a consecrated Religious Sister of Mercy but also serve the Body of Christ as a member of the International Theological Commission.

In hindsight, do you see the hints or seeds of those two callings to live as a Bride of Christ and as a philosopher/academic present in that primary call of Christ to follow him into full communion with his Church?

My life has been full of surprises. Just when I think that I am where God wants me to be, I am called into something new. Early on I thought I would become a Benedictine nun, and in Quebec the monasteries I visited for retreat regularly said they thought I had a religious vocation but not to them. In the meantime, I continued with my teaching and research until I found the right place. Then my younger sister also became Catholic and she entered the Religious Sisters of Mercy of Alma, Michigan. She told the mother general about me, who then invited me to come for a visit. Before long I followed my sister into the RSM postulancy. They decided to open a foundation in Montreal, and in time, I was sent back there to the same philosophy department at Concordia University with a new religious name and a religious habit but now living in a religious community with a superior who taught at McGill University and with other sisters who joined us.

After several years, I took early retirement from Concordia University and was sent to Denver, Colorado with three other Religious Sisters of Mercy and invited to establish a department of philosophy for the intellectual formation of seminarians at what became St. John Vianney Theological Seminary. It was here that I began to love the Church in a new way through participation in the intellectual formation of seminarians and working on the complementarity of philosophy and theology.

When we had completed our work of founding the seminary, I was sent to Lancaster, England to work in the bishop's archives. It was here that I received the letter appointing me to the International Theological Commission as a member from the United States of America. I was stunned and actually thought they had made a mistake. I was a philosopher and not a theologian. When I asked the secretary of the theological commission about this, he told me that they always have three members: a philosopher, an Old Testament scholar, and a New Testament scholar who are able to help as consultants to the theologians.

During this time, I have come to realize that while originally I fell in love with Jesus Christ and the members of the Holy Trinity, I have recently fallen in love with his Church. This leads me to pray often for the Church especially in the midst of crises, turmoil, and betrayals. The wounds of the Church open up to the world the great source of healing and redemption for the whole world.

You've spent a lot of your academic career writing on the philosophy of woman, particularly as expounded upon by Saint John Paul II and Saint Edith Stein. Would you say these two saints played an important role in your conversion story? If not, were there other saints who played a noteworthy role in your journey to the Catholic Church?

When I began my writing about woman's identity in herself and in relation to man, I was just a young lay woman professor looking for something to publish. In those days, the sixties and early seventies, most texts in philosophy (and professors as well) never spoke or wrote about woman as a philosophical subject. This surprised me because both Plato (*Republic* V) and Aristotle (*Metaphysics* X, 9) asked serious questions about it. So I began to write short articles about this topic. Since they easily were accepted for publication,

I continued. I also wrote several articles about the great women religious in Montreal and Quebec history.

To answer your question, my journey to conversion did not come through reading Saint John Paul II or Saint Edith Stein, but once I was a Catholic in Montreal, I read what I could find about them and began to teach their works in different courses and to publish articles on them in the Catholic newspaper. It was during that time that the idea came to me to try to systematically study the history of the concept of woman in relation to man over a sabbatical. I also decided to audit courses in Catholic philosophy at the Catholic University of America to fill in the lack of my background in this area at my secular university studies.

At this time, Pope John Paul II was articulating theories of the complementarity of woman and man in his audiences on *Genesis*. These catecheses came to be known as the "Theology of the Body." These confirmed my own thinking about the subject; namely, that women and men have simultaneous equal dignity and significant difference. He developed the meaning of this principle of integral gender complementarity. I was eager to learn all about it.

It has taken over forty years to complete my four texts on the "Concept of Woman." In these texts I tried to identify all the authors who contributed in some particular way to the historical development of the concept of woman in relation to man. Many of these are Catholic philosophers: both women and men. Several of them are saints. Even though St. John Paul II had the greatest influence on my thought about woman's identity, I came to the conclusion that the truth about woman's identity in relation to man is the result of a communion of scholars, many of whom provide only a part of the whole truth.

These four books that you've authored comprise a seminal series of books on the history of the philosophy of woman. As their subtitles suggest, they're expansive, beginning with Ancient Greece and going all the way to the Modern Day. That's an incredibly daunting task—researching all of the major thinkers in the Western Tradition and then trying to explain their thought on women and how they relate to each other. How did these volumes on "The Concept of Woman" come to fruition?

In the beginning of my work as a young professor in Montreal (the late 1960s), I just wanted to write an article which would get published. My degree was in the history of philosophy with an emphasis on metaphysics and philosophical anthropology (philosophy of the person). I noticed that Aristotle and Kierkegaard had a similar concept of woman but a very different concept of man. This is how it all started.

From there I began to carefully write another paper about a different philosopher's concept of woman (e.g., Plato and then Nietzsche). This was the time when much written about woman was ideological and often polemic. Instead, I wanted to give an accurate description of the concept of woman in the work of the philosopher as a whole. So I used Fr. Copleston's *History of Philosophy* as my model. In this way, the reader (an educated person but not necessarily a philosopher) could understand my paper. When possible, I would first present a draft of the paper in a public lecture or at a conference; next, I would consult with an expert on the author by asking for a critique of any errors before submitting it for publication. Each paper was accepted immediately, so I just kept following this path.

My goal from the beginning was to state what was true about the subject. During this same time frame I was also team-teaching with a colleague in an interdisciplinary women's studies program. We together worked on a framework for this project which we called "women's conceptual history." I was able to present this elemental theory at women's studies conferences, and then published articles about it in a few journals. This started conversations across the country about how to approach women's studies.

When the opportunity for my first sabbatical came (1979), I decided naively to write one book on the whole history of the concept of woman in philosophy in chronological order. What I thought might take me one year actually took forty-five years! I was able to get supportive grants and went to Washington, DC to begin this work. When I got to the Library of Congress to begin with the pre-Socratics, I was shocked to discover that nearly every philosopher had something to say about the topic. We had never studied these writings in undergraduate or graduate school. By October, I requested a second year for my sabbatical and was able to complete volume one as *The Concept of Woman: The Aristotelian Revolution (750 BC to 1250 AD)*.

A structure of the concept of woman in relation of man revealed itself at this early stage of research as containing four dimensions: 1) Are female and male opposite or the same? 2) Does what the mother or father contribute to generation reflect back or not on their human identity? 3) Do women and men have the same or different capacities for wisdom or not? And are they wise by knowing the same or different things? and 4) Do women and men have the same capacity for virtue or not? And are they good by doing the same or different things? Having been a math major before discovering philosophy, I put these four dimensions in a bracket [opposites, generation, wisdom, virtue]. This allowed me to sort my file cards into these four categories as I researched an author.

Two theories began to emerge from the four categories: a unisex theory that answered that there were no significant differences between men and women and a traditional sex polarity theory that answered males were by nature superior to females. Plato and Aristotle were the authors who gave the most thorough answers across all four categories.

Early during these two years of research and writing, Pope John Paul II came to Washington, DC, and I became familiar with his audiences on *Genesis*, which provided a theological perspective on the complementarity of woman and man, the very theory I was working toward in philosophical sources. In his theological analysis, sex complementarity appeared as a third theory which answered that men and women were significantly different but neither the male or the female was superior to the other in all respects. Augustine, Hildegard of Bingen, Dante, and others provided philosophical elements of sex complementarity.

Also, I experienced for the first time the wonderful collegiality of Catholic philosophy professors at the Catholic University of America (CUA). They allowed me to audit classes in areas I needed to learn about and provided valuable critiques of sections of the manuscript. With my grant money, I hired students from CUA to help me in the practical logistics of research and I was given a desk in the stacks of the Library of Congress. These practical gifts made it possible for me to complete the first volume.

From all of this research, who do you see as the major philosophical influencers of our present thinking on women? How would the Church affirm or refute those thinkers' convictions at our moment in history?

The present major influences on our thinking about women have come from the Cartesian and post-Enlightenment traditions. These influences led to a Cartesian influence for a new form of unisex approach which promoted women's education and suffrage and on a religious Reform approach to a fractional complementarity where the woman and man in marriage add up to only one person. This latter position also often held a hidden traditional polarity view inside it. In addition, in the late Renaissance another new theory of reverse sex polarity revealed itself with authors putting forth arguments that women are by nature superior to men. Some of these positions influence radical feminist positions today.

The Renaissance versions of these various positions are described in detail in the second volume, *The Concept of Woman: The Early Humanist Reformation*. In this volume, I introduced the concept of gender and incorporated it into new names for the, by now, four theories of the respective identities of woman and man: gender unity (unisex), traditional gender polarity, reverse gender polarity, and fractional complementarity.

In my third volume, I actually trace the different influences and identified their fundamental (often flawed) foundations and the new developments of solid philosophical foundations, so readers who want to know more on this question should probably consult that volume. Specifically, a wonderful renewal of neo-Thomism provided new foundations for what I tried to prove is the correct position on woman's and man's personal identities and integral complementarity relations. While Thomas Aquinas himself had some serious errors about woman, man, and generation (having followed Aristotle and Albert's erroneous views), contemporary scientists have identified the errors and through the work of neo-Thomists like Maritain, Lonergan, Krapiec, Clarke, Anscombe, and others. Now the metaphysical foundations of the human person provide a key organizing factor to explain how women and men provide significantly different contributions to generation.

The phenomenology of Edith Stein and its development in Lublin Existential Personalism by Karol Wojtyla added many foundational dimensions to what I called "Integral Gender Complementarity." In this theory, a woman and a man are no longer considered as fractional but rather as whole beings, who then in union with one another, generate something more, a third being and/or an intergenerational family. When Karol Wojtyla was elected as Pope John Paul II, Integral Gender Complementarity was then adopted by the universal Church through his own audiences and writings.

These factors are described in the third volume and worked out in more detail in published articles about these authors and others as well. In addition, using Newman's seven criteria for the true development of an idea, in this same volume I attempt to demonstrate that only integral gender complementarity fulfills all seven criteria for a true living idea. In this volume, I seek to provide a comprehensive line of truth about woman and man drawing from the contributions of several scholars, each one of whom provides something true but no one of whom provides all the truth.

To return to your question about how would the Church affirm or refute philosophical influencers of our present thinking on women, the Church usually waits until scholars offer serious critiques of erroneous views on a subject before approving or condemning one position or another. For this reason, it is very important for scholars to present their theories at conferences and to publish them in academic journals and books.

It's interesting, as you mention, that the Church seems very cautious about approving or condemning a particular position on a subject. Even within the Church it seems like there's some positions on the nature of women, positions of canonized saints, where they really disagree. I'm thinking of St. Edith Stein for example, who thought men and women have different souls, whereas Aquinas and strict followers of Aquinas would reject this. Thomists think that gender is an inseparable accident that's present at the level of material but not in the form of the person. Does the difference between men and women go beyond the material in your thinking and has the Church come down clearly on this question on the side of Stein or Aquinas?

One of the central themes I look at in all three volumes of *The Concept of Woman* is the specific arguments of each author about what constitutes the nature of woman and of man. Aristotle correctly stated that empirical science is about "what is always or usually the case." Some human beings are exceptions, but these exceptions do not destroy the rule. This is the error with many theories proposed by Kinsey, Money, Foucault, and others who end up arguing that there is nothing common to women's or men's, or even human, identities and no principle that organizes the person from within.

To answer your question about Edith Stein. While the Church is leaving open the question about women having a different soul from men, most Catholic scholars (myself included) argue that since a soul is the key to a species, and a species is capable of generating itself, this would exclude a woman or a man from being a species by herself or himself. Instead, the best response seems to be the commensuration hypothesis, first suggested by Thomas Aquinas in the *Summa Contra Gentiles* and developed by Msgr. John Wippel and Norris Clarke; namely, that the human soul, when commensurated by God to a particular chromosomal male or female body, will "always or for the most part" develop the human being in some ways allowed by and not other ways limited by this the union of this human soul with its particular body.

During your last answer you also spoke of your theory of "Integral Gender Complementarity." I find myself avoiding the word gender these days because its definition has changed so dramatically, even in the last five years, with the transgender movement. How did this happen? Is there any way to recover its true meaning? Do you foresee a future in the academy where thinkers are able to think and write about women as having a certain nature that is distinct from men, or will that possibility be obliterated by the prevailing ideologies surrounding gender?

I think that scholars in the academy should be free to write about their own theories of sex and/or gender identity. When in the public arena, their arguments and evidence can be studied and affirmed or rebutted. The difficulty today is that certain groups promoting an ideology prefer to shout down their opponents rather than engage in serious and important dialogue.

In contrast, several examples of productive dialogue on these topics can be found throughout history. Many men and women engaged in dialogue about woman's identity together and separately. They wrote examples of dialogue about woman's identity. Sometimes when filled with satire, they ridiculed one another, and other times they worked to achieve a genuine truth. They can offer many examples to us contemporary persons.

I wrote an online article called "Gender reality vs. Gender ideology" which explains my own thoughts on this in more depth that might be helpful to you and others. In addition to tracing the origins of sex ideology (Kinsey), gender ideology (Money), and the paths through which it "went viral" in the world, I also use the word *gender* to describe the whole person distinguished as woman or man. It, therefore, includes the dimension of "sex." Going back to the Western origins, the root of gender or "gen" is found both in Book 5 of *Genesis* and in Aristotle's discussions of "generation" where it means "to breed or reproduce." In the human race, both a male and a female are needed to generate. In the *Generation of Animals,* Aristotle distinguishes the male as one who generates in another and the female as the one who generates in the self. This is a good distinction. These two sources based on faith and reason are accurate and deserve to be kept and developed.

No matter how much various ideologies attempt to kidnap the truth about reality, they will not work. Reality always wins out. It is important for ordinary women and men as well as scholars and academics to ransom gender from gender ideologies and sex from sex ideologies by using the words *gender* and *sex* in the way that they think is true.

T. S. Eliot writes in the "Four Quartets," "In my end is my beginning": so, if you don't mind, I thought we would end where we began—with your conversion story. What advice would you give to souls who are where you once were—tentatively exploring the possibility that the Catholic Church is where the fullness of grace and truth is to be found?

There is no church like the Catholic Church for its universality and its openness to new developments. Newman used

seven criteria to assess true development to prove to himself that the Catholic Church was the true development of
the Church founded by Jesus Christ. 1) Preserve identity
of the original type through all its apparent changes and
vicissitudes from first to last; 2) continuity of development,
changes do not destroy the type; 3) assimilative power (of
dogmatic truth); 4) logical sequence (in fidelity in development); 5) anticipation of its future (in favor of the fidelity
of development, ethical or political); 6) conservative action
on its past (of the original idea) with corruption tending
to its destruction; 7) chronic vigor of a true development
of an idea in distinction from its corruptions, perversions,
and decays.

If the person is seeking an intellectual answer to your
question, the Roman Catholic Church is the only Church
which fills all these seven criteria. Its chronic vigor testifies
to this reality. If the person is seeking instead a personal
experience of the Church, then part of Pascal's wager can
be very helpful. Try it out by attending adoration of the
Blessed Sacrament, attending Church regularly, praying "as
if you believe" in God, ask for the gift of faith, then see
what happens.

Chapter Three

A Swedish Megachurch Pastor and the Rosary

Ulf & Birgitta Ekman

Interviewed by R. J. Snell

Ulf Ekman was born in Gothenburg, Sweden and ordained a Lutheran minister in 1979, first serving as a university chaplain in Uppsala. In 1983 he founded Word of Life, a non-denominational Charismatic church in Uppsala, Sweden and was its Senior Pastor for thirty years. He founded several Bible schools and a seminary, has led conferences and seminars in many nations, including the former USSR, Eastern Europe, and India, and has written more than forty books and booklets, translated into over thirty languages. These include: *Take, Eat (A Book About the Holy Eucharist)*, *A Life of Worship*, *Jesus*, and *Our Holy Calling*.

Birgitta Ekman was born in India, where her parents served as missionaries. For many years she has worked with a foundation she started, IndianChildren, which provides education, food, and health care to many hundreds of Indian children. She has written five illustrated children's books based on her memories of her childhood in India and with Ulf co-authored *The Great Discovery (Den Stora Upptäckten—Vår Väg till Katolska Kyrkan)* about their journey to Rome.

R. J. Snell directs the Center on the University and Intellectual Life at the Witherspoon Institute in Princeton, NJ. Prior to this appointment, he was for many years Professor of Philosophy and Director of the

Philosophy Program at Eastern University and the Templeton Honors College, where he founded and directed the Agora Institute for Civic Virtue and the Common Good. A convert to Catholicism, he grew up Baptist and received his early education at the schools of Prairie Bible Institute and Liberty University. His first encounter with Rome occurred while pursuing an MA in philosophy at Boston College, where he took several courses with Peter Kreeft. Later he earned a PhD in philosophy at Marquette University. He is the author of several books as well as articles, chapters, and essays in a variety of scholarly and popular venues. He and his family reside in the Princeton area.

R. J. Snell: *In writing of your conversion, you remark "how little" you really knew about Catholic belief and piety before exploring it. Some Catholics may not know much about charismatic communities, and your previous Word of Life community in particular. Would you say a bit about the distinctive beliefs and practices of those communities and why they were so attractive to you?*

Ulf & Birgitta Ekman: As a theology student in the early 1970s, while preparing to be a Lutheran minister, I was confronted with liberal theology and the notion of dismissing all supernatural elements of the Scriptures and the Christian faith, with the denial of central dogmas and an eagerness to modernize both ethics and the idea of the church. This created a deep desire in me, as well as in many others, to seek, discover, and experience the reality behind the words of Scripture.

The evangelical student outreaches and the charismatic renewal at that time seemed to me to be a radical answer to these questions. It provided a more central and fresh outlook on Christianity and a passionate commitment. I came from a secularized background and had a strong conversion experience in 1970, so I was not steeped in a particular denominational form.

During my few years as a Lutheran university chaplain

at Uppsala University, serving the evangelical stream of Lutheran students, I saw a big need for more Bible knowledge and evangelistic experience, and out of this came the idea of starting an inter-denominational Bible school, mainly for young people, which I founded in 1983. There was a huge interest in a school like this and it grew quickly. We then also saw a need for a non-denominational charismatic church and it also grew rapidly over the years. The basic tenets of our faith were evangelical with an emphasis of Bible teaching together with a charismatic experience. Faith as a living experience was emphasized and a big missions program started, which after the fall of the Berlin Wall in 1989 resulted in an extensive mission into Russia and Eastern Europe. This created a network of around one thousand new congregations in these nations, over the many years that we worked there.

What appealed to me was the personal walk with Jesus, trusting in the Scriptures as a personal word into our lives. Among us was an expectation that the Lord could and would work miracles today, that the supernatural was real, and that, giving your life to God, you could be led by him into a missions work that actually changed the lives of thousands of people. We believed that the Gospel was the "power of God unto salvation."

You've written on finding a "great love of Jesus and sound theology" in Catholicism. As you were first exploring the Church, what about her theology struck you as most "sound"?

Being part of the evangelical/charismatic movements, I saw that there was a lack, sometimes an open scorn, for the long history of the Church. The understanding of continuity from the past was vague, as we instead emphasized discontinuity—constant new revivals, new local congregations within a congregational and independent ecclesiological understanding. We had a pragmatic look at the present and a futuristic eschatology, sensing that we wanted to "hasten the return of Jesus Christ."

We had a typical "sola Scriptura" understanding of the Bible, with a very low ecclesiological understanding of structure, hierarchy, and magisterium. The sacramental life was missing. So, more than anything else, it was the sacramental element that started to draw me towards the Catholic Church.

So, during the last ten years I was a Protestant pastor, I perceived many pieces were missing. What struck me about the Catholic Church were its inner order, harmony, and stability. I found that the theology was so clear, sound, and well thought through. It was rational but still faithful. I would say four words could summarize what I found so appealing: historicity, apostolic continuity, authority, and sacramentality.

It was also surprising to us, in the encounter with many Catholics, how their love for Jesus was shining through and how the clergy—the priests we met and even the pope— spoke so freely and boldly about Jesus Christ. We had not expected that.

You've also written that the Church exhibited the moral strength and consistency "that dare to face up to the general opinion." Could you say a bit more about what you mean? Also, many Catholics disagree with the Church on various moral teachings. From the perspective of a convert, what counsel would you give them?

What attracted me, especially contrasted with more liberal elements of Protestantism, was the strength of holding onto traditional dogma in a time where the whole idea about dogma was depreciated. The Catholic Church is a clear and outspoken voice in morals and ethics and to discover this was refreshing. In Pope John Paul II, I discovered to my surprise the combination of modern outlook and missions initiative with a strong classical theological foundation, going back over the centuries, with a passionate appeal for holiness. The teaching on the dignity of man, the culture of life, sexual morals, and the protection of the unborn child were all very appealing to me.

Being a part of and living in a secularized culture and a liberal protestant milieu that constantly accommodates to the latest ideas, I saw how relativism actually destroyed much of the fibers of the faith. Of course, there were also in our circles elements of a type of narrow conservatism that bordered on judgmental spiritual elitism and an enclave mentality.

But in the Catholic Church I saw the possibility to be true and passionate without being sectarian or accommodating to worldliness. There existed the tools and the culture to live a more true, full, and compassionate Christian life, much due to the sacramental life that protects us from going off-center. The balance of different important elements was important to me.

Prior to a deeper encounter with the Church, you've described yourselves as having "Protestant prejudices," sometimes without much basis. Which preconceptions were you most surprised to find incorrect? Why are these Protestant preconceptions so prevalent?

As a Swedish Protestant many prejudices came with the cultural air we breathe. Sweden has been one of the most staunchly Protestant nations in the world. Today it is secularized, but beneath a thin veneer of relativistic modernism there are still deeply held Protestant beliefs, even influencing agnostics and atheists in their view of the Catholic Church. In our culture there is an anti-Catholic sentiment that runs deep since the Reformation. It has surfaced again—more among Protestant Christians than in the general population, I would say—since there has recently been a number of conversions to the Catholic Church, mine included. There are different layers of misconceptions about the Catholic Church: Lutheran prejudices, Evangelical Free Church prejudices, cultural and socialistic prejudices. The Social Democratic party, which has dominated governmental power for decades, has been notoriously skeptical about the Catholic Church.

Taking all this into account, although some things are clearly changing, makes it a bit hard for the common man to understand or appreciate the Catholic Church, at least at first glance. Although, I must say that the last few years there has been a notable change; Swedes are now more curious in their attitude. Pope Francis visited Sweden in 2016, the canonization of the second ever Swedish saint, Mary Elizabeth Hesselblad, also occurred in 2016, and the creation of the first ever Swedish cardinal, Bishop Anders Arborelius in 2017. These three "Catholic news" stories have indeed caught the eyes of both the media and the public in quite a positive way.

The most prevalent theological prejudices, or lack of knowledge, would be the ideas about the pope as an Anti-Christ, prayers offered to Mary and veneration of the saints as some form of idolatry, purgatory as a "second chance" after death, and Tradition as making Scripture null and void. There is a constant accusation that says the Catholic Church teaches salvation through works, and many Swedes still see the Church as a dead structure with an oppressing hierarchy, which hinders the "freedom of the Spirit."

Especially the idea about oppressing women by the denial of women priests preoccupies the minds of media as well as the general public. The forbidding of the use of contraceptives and being against abortion, as well as the view of homosexual acts as sin and the forbidding of divorced to re-marry seems medieval, outlandish, and something that should not be permitted in a modern society, et cetera, et cetera.

I've read that the Lord "gave you a word" which assisted you in converting. Would you explain that a bit more? When you look back at your journey to Rome, how much of it was motivated by intellectual conviction, how much by spiritual leading? How do you understand the relationship between the intellect and the guidance of the Holy Spirit? Has your understanding of that relationship developed or altered since becoming Catholic?

As Christians we have all received the Holy Spirit through baptism. I do think this is a matter of being taught and encouraged to understand and dare to open up to the Holy Spirit, who resides in us. He is willing to help, lead, and to speak to us, both through our intellect, through the Magisterium, through the Scriptures, and as many saints give witness to, an inner impression or still small voice in our heart. My wife, Birgitta, and I constantly studied, searched, and discussed the possibility of actually finding the truth existing in the Catholic faith. It was an experience on many levels. There is an intellectual challenge, a cultural challenge, and an experiential challenge. I needed help on all levels.

As our journey started I had an impression, a sentence that surfaced in my mind: "Get to know the Essence of the Church." The word *essence* in terms of the Church was a concept that I had to discover. I was much more familiar with the beliefs, the actions, the mission of the Church, et cetera. In my heart I was also meditating on four other words, "get to know the Church," "appreciate it," "draw closer to it," and "unite with it." These words became like a program, a formula for me during ten years of intellectual searching. As we started to come close to make a decision, I woke up one night with a very clear sense of a personal word to me: "It is time to jump into the waters. You can go the way of Jonah or the way of Peter, but it is time to go into the water."

For me this was a clear call, after some considerable procrastination, to join the Catholic Church. I had no theological problems at all at this time, but what about the responsibility of my pastoral ministry? This sense of responsibility had kept me back, but now I had conviction to move on. I do believe this was the leading of the Holy Spirit, and now as I look back I am very happy I was led this way as it also meant a lot to people in my circles when I gave testimony about how the Lord has lead us.

You have resisted what you once termed a "postmodern" under-standing whereby one thinks something like "Ok, I'm Catholic, but I'll choose to believe or not believe this or that doctrine of the Church." Instead, you write that "to be Catholic actually means to believe as a Catholic." What does it mean to "believe as a Catholic"?

Upon coming into the Catholic Church, I was confront-ed by many of my friends. Some of them did not have a huge problem with me becoming Catholic, but they did not really believe that I accepted all the teachings of the Church. To them I had to repeatedly say, "As a Catholic I do believe as a Catholic." I do believe, not just a creed or certain selective tenets of the faith, but everything the

Church teaches. This is what one promises when one is received into the Church. That came as a shock to some of my friends. During the almost fifteen years we were drawn closer to the Church, I think I read the Catechism three times all through and numerous times opened up to different passages for more clarity. For me the Catechism became the standard of what I should believe and a door into the teachings of the Magisterium.

What about Catholic practice and piety were you surprised to find life-giving? For example, I was taken completely off-guard by the powerful experience of Eucharistic Adoration. Do you have any similar experiences? What about Catholic life and piety, if anything, still feels a bit strange or unexpected?

The Catholic Church has a culture that in one way is quite alien to the Protestant mindset, but, when you get to know it, it is very refreshing. But it does take time. Popular piety appealed to me because during my whole life as a pastor I have been working with laity. What surprised us was the fervor and strength of Marian piety. It took us a while to understand how important this was. We decided to visit some Marian shrines, and over the years, we visited Lourdes, Fatima, Knock, Guadalupe, Czestochowa, Banneux, as well as many churches and monasteries connected with Mary. The Rosary started to appeal to us when we realized how Christ-centered it is, and we started to pray the Rosary even before we were received into the Church. I can't really think of anything still being "strange or unexpected."

Prior to forming Word of Life, you were Lutherans, I understand. Given that background, I imagine that the doctrine of justification by faith alone was important, even vital, to you. How do you understand that doctrine now? Does it remain a real difference between the Church and Protestants? If yes, how? If not, why not?

I used to believe the four "sola" tenets of the Reformation, about Scripture, Faith, Grace, and Jesus Christ, more or less out of Protestant habit or tradition. Step-by-step I started to see how the Protestant mindset has an overriding attitude of "either-or" while the Catholic mindset, as well as the Hebrew, is more of "both-and." By omitting the word *sola/only* things become clearer. By looking at works/deeds in the light of "corresponding actions" and how grace and faith cooperates, it makes much more sense and the writings of the apostle James does not become contradictory to that of the apostle Paul, but complementary. As there are many Scripture passages that clearly emphasize the importance of works or deeds for our salvation, it became clear that "sola fide" is not correct.

It was also surprising, but pleasing to us, that the Catholic Church and the Lutheran World Federation came to a common understanding about the controversy of the doctrine of Justification in 1999, which thereby ended that conflict. But I am not sure of how many there are who actually know about this document and quote it in public discussions. And yes, there are many Protestants who do not accept this agreement. There is still a real difference between Catholic and Protestant thought in these matters. At least in my former circles there is with some people a real fear of anything that smells of "works," and some even say that any form of "righteousness through works" destroys our possibility to be saved. Among some, the fear of finding oneself outside of real faith, in doing something out of wrong intentions or believing something doctrinally wrong, is very tangible and creates a very suspicious and spiritually unsound lifestyle. Others are very laidback and think nothing can separate them from salvation because God loves them just as they are.

A directly personal question, if I may. You've been described as the "most dynamic and influential Christian leader" in Sweden in decades. Obviously you've continued to offer your talents and heart to the Church and to Christians of all sorts, and yet I imagine that there were difficulties in leaving ordained ministry. I have friends, for instance, formerly Protestant pastors, who found it a significant emotional challenge to become a parishioner in the pews rather than the shepherd. How did you find the courage and humility to do this?

Yes, of course it was quite difficult to leave the ministry but it was also very satisfying, as there was such an inner hunger in us and a desire to be united with the Catholic Church. But naturally we had to handle the quite intense opposition that followed our conversion. We came into a different spiritual landscape and needed our quiet time to get acquainted. Personally I needed this because my intense work had led to overexertion in 2012. After many years of intense ministry, it was such a rare and wonderful gift to be able to pause a while and to be able to reflect and rest a bit more.

We have now been "ordinary parishioners" for some years. It is quite satisfying not to be in charge of every service, every activity, not having to answer every call and constantly talk to a stream of people. But we have also been quite busy in another way, having been writing and traveling quite a lot internationally and also having informal study groups with old friends and others who have been interested in getting to know more about the Catholic faith. Some of them have also joined the Catholic Church.

Chapter Four

The Harvard Law Professor and "A Great Lady"

Adrian Vermeule

Interviewed by Christina Deardurff

Adrian Vermeule is the Ralph S. Tyler Professor of Constitutional Law at Harvard Law School. A graduate of Harvard College ('90) and Harvard Law School ('93), he served as a law clerk for the late Justice Antonin Scalia in 1994–95, and has authored or co-authored eight books, including *Law's Abnegation: From Law's Empire to the Administrative State.*

Christina Deardurff is Assistant Editor at the monthly print journal *Inside the Vatican.* She is an alumna of Thomas Aquinas College in Santa Paula, California, and the mother of ten.

Christina Deardurff: *Could you cite those who influenced your interest in and decision to convert to Catholicism? What is your previous religious background?*

Adrian Vermeule: I was baptized and raised as an Episcopalian/Anglican; my first school was run by Anglican nuns and I later attended an historically Episcopalian boarding school. I fell away from the Episcopal Church in college, and when I returned in later life, it was a different place.

There are many "small-O" orthodox Christians remaining within it, including dear friends, but they have lost control of the institution to heterodox forces.

As for influences, there were many, especially Cardinal Newman, Father Brian Dunkle, SJ, Father Kevin Grove, CSC, who generously arranged my reception at Notre Dame, a set of lay and clerical scholars and friends from Notre Dame, Harvard, and other universities, friends at St. Paul Parish at Harvard, and a larger cloud of witnesses throughout the Church. But behind and above all those who helped me along the way, there stood a great Lady.

Did you experience any kind of mystical or possibly supernatural signs or occurrences relating to your conversion?

Let me refer back to the end of the previous answer and leave it at that.

What is the logic of your Catholic position against the present zeitgeist? How could you choose the Catholic faith in our time—a time of turmoil in the Church and evident sin among Catholics, even the clergy?

The intellectual logic is unoriginal and Newman-derived. Raised a Protestant, despite all my thrashing and twisting, I eventually couldn't help but believe that the apostolic succession, through Peter as the designated leader and *primus inter pares*, is in some logical or theological sense prior to everything else—including even Scripture, whose formation was guided and completed by the apostles and their successors, themselves inspired by the Holy Spirit. A corollary is the very great evil of schism and private judgment, brought home to me when the Episcopal Church essentially decided to go its own way based on novel views, even in the face of faithful admonition by the broader Anglican Communion. Ultimately I think with Newman—and with the Notre Dame historian Brad Gregory, whose brilliant book *The Unintended Reformation* crystallizes the idea—that there is no stable middle ground between Catholicism and atheist materialism. One must always be traveling, or slipping unintentionally, in one direction or the other.

As for a "time of turmoil" in the Church, I'm not convinced that's true. Or, to put it differently, it's always true in greater or lesser degree, but the depths of the Church are not disturbed by the storms that pass to and fro on the surface. Perhaps I speak now with the naiveté and enthusiasm of the convert, but the Church seems to me an institution whose foundations are as strong as iron. The turmoil will pass away; episodes, scandals and debates will come and go; but the line and witness of Peter's successors will never fail.

Which saints do you admire and learn from? Augustine? Thomas More? John Henry Newman?

Athanasius, Aquinas (especially for his political and legal theory; parochial of me, I know, but each sentence cuts like a razor), Joan of Arc, Newman, and the profound psychologist Josemaria Escrivá. But most of all, nearest to my heart, a young and fiercely courageous Jewish refugee girl who teaches inexhaustible lessons, Miriam bat Joachim.

Do you think the West can still be called "Christian" or did that end a long time ago? Is there hope for a religious renewal in the West? How?

There is hope for renewal, because of Father Jacques Hamel and others like him. God acts through the weak and the marginal—the humble aged parish priest who goes to his death filled with faith and courage, naming the darkness and pushing it away. Out of this, God has fashioned a light to illuminate France and the whole West.

On what legal fronts do you find the most hope for influencing the culture away from the "culture of death" of materialism and nihilism we seem to be gradually embracing?

I put little stock or hope or faith in law. It is a tool that may be put to good uses or bad. In the long run it will be no better than the polity and culture in which it is embedded. If that culture sours and curdles, so will the law; indeed that process is well underway and its tempo is accelerating. Our hope lies elsewhere.

This interview originally appeared in the October 2016 issue of Inside the Vatican. *Used with permission.*

Chapter Five

A Searcher Discovers Thomas Aquinas

Fr. Thomas Joseph White, OP

Interviewed by Hope Kean

Thomas Joseph White, OP, grew up in southeast Georgia in an inter-religious household. He studied at Brown University and Oxford University and entered the Order of Preachers in 2003. He is the director of the Thomistic Institute at the Angelicum in Rome and a professor of theology. Among his books are included *Wisdom in the Face of Modernity: A Study in Thomistic Natural Theology, The Incarnate Lord: A Thomistic Study in Christology,* and *The Light of Christ: An Introduction to Catholicism.* In 2011 he was appointed an ordinary member of the Pontifical Academy of St. Thomas Aquinas.

Hope Kean, a convert herself, graduated from Princeton University in 2018. She is a member of Princeton's Aquinas community and a student member of the Thomistic Institute, part of the Dominican House of Studies in Washington, DC.

Hope Kean: *What is your current role in the Catholic Church?*

Fr. Thomas Joseph White: I'm a Catholic priest in the Dominican Order and teach theology and philosophy at the Dominican House of Studies. I also direct the

Thomistic Institute which puts on academic conferences at secular university campuses. We try to bring Catholic intellectual content to the venues where it's not typically accessible. [Editor's note: Since this interview, Fr. White has taken up a new position at the Pontifical University of St. Thomas Aquinas, the Angelicum, in Rome.]

What was your religious upbringing, if any?

I grew up in southeast Georgia as the only child of a Jewish father and a Presbyterian mother. My parents were nominally or moderately religious. My father could be characterized as a somewhat secularized Jew and my mother was a modestly practicing Presbyterian, so I had some exposure to both traditions but was neither baptized nor Bar Mitzvah-ed. And, of course, I'm not Jewish in the Jewish understanding of the term because that passes through the lineage of the mother. I was surrounded by many people who were deeply Protestant or committed Southern Baptists in southeast Georgia, but I was a sort of generic theist without any real personal awareness of Christ. I did not consider myself an atheist by any means but the existence of God wasn't a concern of great importance. I did pray as a child, even up into my early adolescence, but I wouldn't say I was very self-consciously prayerful or particularly reflective about religious matters. When I was maybe ten or eleven, we traveled a great deal in Asia which gave me an interest in religious diversity. I remember wanting to understand the fundamental differences between religions, what you might call a premature metaphysical curiosity, but it wasn't religious practice, it was more like a concern about religious truth. By high school I was pretty unconcerned with religious issues, but then I went to boarding school at Phillips

Academy in Andover which eventually precipitated a kind of religious crisis or question . . . questioning.

Did your religious upbringing influence what you chose to study at boarding school?

At school I encountered an intensive and self-conscious secularism leading to the typical culture shock of a person coming from a rural, religious background into a culture where there's a high degree of self-conscious atheism and secularism. That raised questions for me about what I thought about life. Like many academically inclined people in late adolescence, I was primarily thinking through the prism of literature. Reading Joyce, *Portrait of the Artist* and *Dubliners*, some Nietzsche, the Romantic Poets, but also American Transcendentalists, was how I asked about meaning. Through this I became interested in the possibility of religious explanations of the world.

Were the other students similarly interested?

The general impression I had was no. My experience there, and later at Brown University, was that most students thought religious ideas were uninteresting or unimportant; perhaps that's unfair, but it seemed like those questions had a muted resonance with them. It struck me as strange that there wasn't an inherent curiosity about the possibility of a religious explanation of reality, even if not a Christian, Jewish, or monotheistic explanation. Something other than a sheer materialist positivism or modern existentialist stance. I was metaphysically perplexed and certainly met some others who were, but it was not typically a prevalent concern.

The chaplain at Andover gave me Martin Buber's *I and*

Thou to read. It had a very big effect on me because I
began to consider that the ultimate mystery in reality could
be something personal. Until then, I presupposed that the
deepest core of reality was basically impersonal, and per-
sonhood, to put it in terms I might use now, was an epiphe-
nomenon, a sort of passing current that would eventually
evaporate. In reading Buber I got the idea that you could
come to know God personally.

My freshman year in college I took a class on Buddhist
and Indian Vedantic metaphysics and was thinking about
the causes of reality. Because I was interested in Eastern
mysticism, I thought I should probably also study Western mysticism, so I started reading Thomas Merton, in
part because he was interested in both. Because of that,
I got interested in things like the Jesus prayer and Christian forms of meditation. It came to my attention that by
meditating on the mystery of God and Christ in one's own
innermost self, you could encounter Christ.

At about the same time, a friend gave me a book of Flan-
nery O'Connor's letters, whom I liked because I'm also
from southeast Georgia. In reading her letters, I encountered a Catholic intellectual. I found her views startlingly
absolutist; shockingly, even offensively so, but also plausible or attractive. I read especially the *Letters to A,* which I
found compelling, in which she mentioned a few theologians, including Karl Barth. So I went to the library
and got out some books of his, including *Introduction to
Evangelical Theology.* I sat in the basement of the Science
Library on Thayer Street, under atrocious fluorescent lights
in this rather awful modern architectural setting, and read
the book virtually cover to cover in an afternoon and evening—when I closed the book, I knew Jesus Christ existed.
That was when I received the gift of faith from God and

began to be aware of the reality of Christ. I went back to my dorm and prayed and the next day went to the college chaplain, who was Protestant, and asked to be baptized.

I was eventually baptized as a Protestant at Easter my freshman year, at which time it became evident that it is very challenging to identify the truth about Christianity because there are lots of different versions of it. I became interested in the nature of Christianity and started going to different churches. I'd sit in the back of Presbyterian churches and go to the high Anglican services, things like this. The next semester I took a class on Early Christianity, thinking that if I studied the historical genesis of Christianity, I would figure out what it was at the beginning. In that class, we were exposed to authors like Ignatius of Antioch and Irenaeus and Augustine and Athanasius, including his important book *On the Incarnation*, and figures like John Chrysostom. As I read them, I had a rising instinct that whatever these authors were articulating, it was something very like Eastern Orthodoxy or Roman Catholicism, like what Newman means when he says that to be deep in history is to cease to be Protestant. As I read the Church Fathers, it became clear that they had a unique combination of philosophical depth, theological profundity, and spiritual mysticism that was beautiful, strange, because ancient, but also powerful and compelling. It seemed to be what the Catholic Church promotes, and it made Catholic things that had previously seemed very strange seem much more attractive—like the sacraments, iconography, the Virgin Mary, the place of the bishops and the papacy, and especially the Eucharist. I started sitting in the back of the Catholic Church and began reading more Church Fathers, especially Origen and Augustine.

Not long after this class had begun, I came across a book

called *Introduction to Christianity*, thinking, "well this is what I need, an introduction." It was written by a person named Joseph Ratzinger. He differed from Barth in emphasizing the combination of philosophy and theology, which I found appealing. I started reading Balthasar, Rahner, de Lubac, and especially John Paul II. Reading them I felt a deep continuity between the Early Fathers and the modern Christianity I was engaging with intellectually. You can imagine all this happening at Brown University when I shared almost no intellectual interests with my fellow students, with whom conversations were about postmodernism, Nietzsche, Foucault, post-Kantian intellectual history, contemporary and modern literature, gender studies, and feminism. In certain ways, that's a totally different world, or at least I didn't have a public setting to engage what I thought was most interesting or important.

In my senior year, I starting reading John Henry Newman and went on a retreat at St. Mary's monastery in Massachusetts, a Subiaco congregation Benedictine monastery. There I met monks from England and Scotland who understood this intellectual tradition I was interested in and who had a high degree of intellectual acumen, but one also grounded in a life of prayer and work. I was surprised by the discovery of people who had this similar interest, also very pleased, and had the strange feeling I had discovered "my tribe" in this little monastery in the woods with Gregorian chant and beautiful solemn liturgy. During my visits there I began to experience Eucharistic Adoration in which I had an overwhelming sense of the presence of Christ that I had never had before, accompanied by an acute awareness of my own sinfulness, but also a radiant sense of the presence and goodness of God. That was overwhelming and powerful, so when I returned to Providence from one of my visits to the monastery, I asked to enter RCIA and was eventually received on Easter Day, 1993, at St. Mary's monastery. It was also at this monastery that I had the firm—and very frightening—sense that I was called to religious life. I broke down crying explaining this to one of the monks, and he said, "It's a good sign that you feel afraid because it's not within the natural power of the human being to live religious life; it's a gift, it's a calling, it's a work of Grace." He also told me I needed a couple of years as a Catholic before I could enter religious life.

You discovered the Dominican order during your time at Oxford, studying for an MPhil in patristic theology?

Oxford was a great time of growth for me as a young person trying to become devout and live my intellectual life as a Catholic. I was helped there by Dominicans and Jesuits. My spiritual director at the time was Michael Barber, a Jesuit, who was the graduate chaplain, who is now the bishop of Oakland, California. I also engaged with the liturgy at the Oratory and soon got to know Oratorian fathers and also became good friends with some of the Dominicans. The Dominicans were influential because of their lectures at Blackfriars, and the young Dominicans seemed to have acute arguments in the domains of philosophy and theology. I noticed that the Dominican intellectual charism was to argue, to identify the harmonies between faith and reason. Whether we were talking about Old and New Testament, historical-critical scholarship and Catholic dogma, modern science and philosophical belief in God, evolutionary theory and the spiritual soul of man, complex bioethical questions and how they relate to human action, or the relationship between the dogmas of the Catholic Church and the historical development of the Church's understanding of them, I found an intellectually rich set of answers that deeply affected me. Modern disciples of Aquinas were using his principles to make sense of the world in ways I found very reasonable and which harmonized commonsense, philosophical profundity, divine revelation, and spiritual mysticism.

When you were grappling with philosophical questions before your conversion, what was the biggest sticking point?

I had the standard undergraduate formation of the early '90s, one indebted to Nietzsche and Foucault, but which also turns toward American liberalism. I would call it a kind of politics of identity, strongly affected by Foucault and Rawls. This is what I was effectively educated in, and those ideas continue to be at the heart of our cultural intellectual life. I had a lot of questions about whether the intellect reaches the truth, the metaphysical constitution of reality, and if we have certitude about that. Is there any such thing as natural knowledge of God? What are the principles by which we begin to articulate a universal human morality, or what are the fundamental principles by which we begin to identify the structures of the natural laws in ourselves? Those questions were left largely unresolved.

At Oxford I began to pose questions about the intelligibility of reality as it relates to the theological truths of the Faith. While I didn't have many resources in myself on that set of questions because I was studying theology rather than philosophy, I knew people who did have a synthetic vision and realized there was a tradition that could grapple with these topics. I had read Alasdair MacIntyre, who engages the Thomistic tradition, so I wanted to study Aquinas more formally, although my access to him was through talking to Dominicans. It was only when I entered seminary that I had a formation in Aristotelian and Thomistic thought.

You've written how people's worldviews are shaped by "a diverse but converging set of unified theories which define one's prior assumptions about what reality is." Is this true of atheists and religious believers alike, and did you fully grasp two sets, as it were, and then determine what was most compelling?

St. Thomas's philosophy of nature, metaphysics, understanding of the human person, epistemology, logic, and ethics make sense even independently of divine revelation while being deeply compatible with it. He also articulates an understanding of revelation which assimilates his realistic philosophical approach to the world. Of course, it's not that you can just read Aquinas and then never have to read anything else or that he provides a system resolving every problem. He does not offer a system but insights into the structure of reality that you can see is true. Simple examples like the distinction between form and matter, for instance, grapple with the fact that a water molecule is different than a kangaroo which is different from a cactus which differs from a human, but still each of them have material elements and component parts present that allow us to understand what they are and how they exist. You can't reduce an explanation of these physical realities to their material component parts or to their essential form. This metaphysical grammar allows you to analyze reality in all physical things. That's just one example, but there are lots of other ones too, and they help you understand so much about the world independently of the Catholic faith. But once you understand them and how they relate to the Faith, you have a very powerful combination. Aquinas is a deeply grounded philosophical realist, a deeply grounded theological realist, and a mystic; it's a very powerful combination.

You found that harmony compelling in St. Thomas and also in the Thomists you met?

Yes, and as I met more people I realized Thomism is a living culture in the Church. It's a mistake to think the Church cannot accommodate a multiplicity of different philosophers and theologies. The Church is united doctrinally, sacramentally, and by its moral ethos, and that real unity can accommodate diverse visions of theology within itself without any rupture, so long as diverse theologies are each receptive of the complete doctrinal teaching of the Church. It's constructive that the members of the Church can argue about philosophy and history, and engage with the study of science and history. Not everybody has to be a Thomist, but it is vital to the Church that there is a Thomistic tradition and culture which is not only a culture of intellect but also a way of life. Aquinas lived the Dominican life of prayer, study, commentary on Sacred Scripture, Eucharistic devotion, deep loyalty to Christ and the Virgin Mary, and service to his brothers—this was all part of how he lived the intellectual life. Of course many people are genuine Thomists without being Dominicans, but the deeper point is that Thomism is an intellectual tradition at the heart of the Church in a living relation with God and in service to others, both through teaching of the truth, which Aquinas calls the greatest spiritual work of mercy, but also through acts of prayer and charity. Aquinas has a profound and beautiful analysis of what the life of service consists in. So, yes, over time I discovered the Thomistic tradition of analysis and also a way of life that is wonderful, present in the Dominican Order.

In your book The Light of Christ, *you write about "a non-Christian monotheist who confides himself to God in poverty of heart or seeks to live by authentic truths of natural law outside of the Catholic Church." Is this an insight you gained only after living the life of a Catholic inside the Church?*

I was writing about the possibility of salvation outside the Church. First of all, the Church teaches unequivocally that salvation occurs only by virtue of the grace of Christ, but my point in that passage is that the grace of Christ can be at work in people who don't explicitly recognize Christ or the truth of Christianity. I'm not being Pelagian in saying this; like Pius IX in the nineteenth century, I'm recognizing that God's grace can be at work in persons of good will. As a priest, I work with people becoming Christian as well as Catholic, so I'm privileged to observe the recurrent dynamic patterns that emerge in people who are evidently affected by grace. Often I work with them with respect to their emotional or ethical challenges, but also with respect to their intellectual challenges to certain Catholic dogmas or teachings. It does seem to me that God's grace is often at work in people who are just seeking to figure out the meaning of life, prior to their decision to be baptized or become Catholic. It's not at all rare for me, for example, to meet with an atheist, or perhaps a person who's Jewish or Muslim or a lapsed ex-Protestant or ex-Catholic, who's intellectually drifting but curious and trying to figure things out. You often see signs or indications of the effects of grace—it's easier to say with confidence that, yes, obviously, grace has been at work here once they move on to seek Baptism or Confirmation.

Generally speaking, do you find conversion to be purely the repudiation of past beliefs and the acceptance of Catholic truth, or is there usually some way in which past beliefs are reinterpreted or integrated into a person's faith?

People convert to Catholicism without retaining a strong awareness of their past musings and experiences. They bring those things into their Catholic understanding of the world in ways that respect the truth of their past experiences and reflections, reinterpreting them in a way that preserves the realism and truth of those experiences rather than denying the truth of previous understanding. Even beliefs that one might later consider erroneous are thought to have contained partial truth. The challenge is trying to figure out what is that partial truth, if it's really true, and if Christ is real, and the teaching of the Catholic Church is true. If the teaching of the Church is true, then in light of that standard, there is a way to judge partial truths in other previously held beliefs, and then there's a way in which one can achieve coherence. In that sense, I would call the process of becoming Catholic assimilative more than it is destructive—the only thing that gets destroyed is the privation of sinfulness and error. Sin is itself a privation of a right order to the good. Error is a privation of the truth. In conversion there is more life not less; more truth not less; a deeper order of well-being rather than less order. And in that you bring along all of the positive good of your person and experience now assimilated to your life in Christ. At times, that can be accomplished through radical renunciation of aspects of life, even if they are legitimate, like, for instance, you *could* sell everything you own to follow Christ even though it's not required. It is not a commandment but a counsel to sell everything and follow Christ, not everyone is called to it, but Christ does call some to it, as he did the rich young man in *Mark*. That's not to destroy the natural good of human existence, but to live out the natural good in a way that's more radically freeing in view of the final end that one aspires to, which is union with Christ in eternal life.

In reclaiming partial truths, should we stress the coherence of Catholic teaching with modern science, or is it more important to show the internal consistency of the Faith?

They're both important priorities in different ways. It's vital to show the harmony of faith with natural science because our culture is so invested in the sciences as an especially trusted form of knowledge. It may not be the most important form, ultimately, but it is primary as the ecumenical consensus in our culture as to what real knowledge is. People think modern scientific knowledge is real knowledge. All other claims to higher knowledge—philosophical, religious, theological—*do* need to be able to show that they can explain themselves in relation to the truths of the natural sciences in order to win people over to a larger understanding. The natural sciences themselves do not give a comprehensive understanding of reality. They can't tell you what justice is. They can't tell you why artistic beauty matters. They can't tell you what the subject of metaphysics is. Or why the world exists, or even if the world is meaningless. The modern natural sciences are always bound in some way by quantitative measurements, and study of the quantitative features of reality alone can't tell you about other aspects of being. So there's a harmony, a great alliance, between natural science and philosophy and theology that needs to be well articulated.

Internal coherence matters too. You can't believe in Revelation if it's inherently anti-intellectual simply on the basis of the teachings and propositions of a religion, especially with regards to the sources of Revelation. There's a question of rational coherence to be raised because we need to be concerned about religious truth.

In Catholic theology, one seeks to show the coherence of the distinct mysteries: that of the Trinity, the Incarnation, the Church, the Eucharist, the Virgin Mary. This coherence is what nineteenth-century theologians called the *Analogia Fidei*, the analogy of faith—the different mysteries relate to one another and they also illumine human realities. But theology is more than a search for internal coherence. It is that, but it's also a kind of practice of insight; I don't know exactly how else to explain it except as something like what Aquinas would call the *habitus* of *intellectus*. It's a speculative *habitus* of the intellect by which we gain insight into the essence of things. Aquinas thinks this is at the heart of our natural intellectual life, aided by the Holy Spirit's gift of understanding (in Latin *intellectus*). The mind is moved by the Holy Spirit to penetrate into the mystery and understand it. That's the highest work of the intellect in this life, made possible by grace and our cooperation with it. In its depths, sacred theology is the attempt to habitually gain insight into the depth and coherence of the mysteries. Above that there's the gift of wisdom, a higher contemplative insight, not the thematic exploration we call theology but a higher mystical engagement through an elevated seeing under the veil of faith. That's the kind of special insight God gives the saints and others so they can live in friendship with God. So you have kind of philosophical search for the truth, you have theological search for the truth, and you have this higher mystical wisdom, but they each anticipate or are harmonious with the other.

Catholic theology seeks to show how truths of natural science and philosophy can be harmonized with

Revelation, and how Revelation in its internal coherence invites us into this contemplative gaze that God the Holy Spirit alone can give us. This vision of three wisdoms— philosophical, theological, mystical—is what you find in Aquinas and what modern Thomists write about with great acuity. It allows you to think about the compatibility of other bodies of knowledge with classical Catholic philosophical and theological learning.

In many ways Thomism is an old way of looking at things that can be foreign to modern thinkers. You write in The Light of Christ *how modern Christianity can sometimes want to gloss over aspects from medieval theology that might be unpopular (like the fear of hell or other more jarring things).*

The Church doesn't just practice remembering, she also practices forgetting. When the Church insists we hold on to our inheritance, she reminds us that while there are many things we can let go of, some things we can never abandon. For instance, the Last Things that you mention: final judgment, hell, purgatory, and heaven. The Church says, yes, there are medieval ways of thinking about these topics that are contingent or debatable, but the realities in question are real and we must call them to mind. These eschatological teachings designate realities that are our own future; we will come under the final judgment of God and are subject the constraints and possibilities of that judgment. We're invited to avoid hell and find heaven, a view that isn't typically welcome among our secular contemporaries, but which has implications for them as well as us. The "gentlemen's agreement" of secular liberalism is that we ought not attempt to find public consensus upon questions of life after death or the dogmatic truth content of revealed religion. In some ways dogma is considered impolite in a secular context because it could be seen as politically or socially divisive. Although the opposite is true in some real sense because dogma tends to outlive many passing cultures and is a force of unity, vitality, and the renewal of intellectual life. Thinking through traditional dogmas invites us as modern people to think about the longstanding vitality of those doctrines—why they're pertinent to persons throughout time and history and a stimulus for the intellectual life. Knowledge of what was profound wisdom in a forgone era is typically the best source of illumination for anyone who wishes to rearticulate the conditions of meaning for the future. The temptation in our own age is to think the opposite, as if we need to be in some kind of radical rupture with the past in order to articulate the conditions of meaning for the future. This is a pattern you find in Descartes or in the opening pages of Kant's *Critique of Pure Reason* or in Nietzsche in a more radical way. But you have people who tend to be both novel and preserve the past; I think this is true of Plato. Plato was very radical, but he also wanted to preserve the heritage of the past Greek religious traditions that came before him. Aristotle, too, is typically very careful in the first book of most of his works to show the insights that come before him and then he introduces a new order of learning and thinking. In general the great medievals like Bonaventure and Aquinas show how the past has contributed to the ongoing project of what they're undertaking. In our own era Alasdair MacIntyre has been exemplary in showing how this kind of recovery and articulation of principles allows renewed engagement with the contemporary world around oneself.

I think Thomism functions best as an identification of principles and an engagement with contemporary intellectual questions.

Which contemporary or modern sentiments or questions do you think Thomas can address?

I may be optimistic, but I think there are many. Thomism helps provide a realistic philosophy of nature, what it means that there are changing substances around us that have identifiable properties by which we can provide taxonomies for the natures of things and understand the ways in which they act upon each other. Aquinas is a phenomenal student of human nature, so he takes very seriously man's physicality and animality, but also shows his emergent rational properties and freedom in their distinctiveness. He shows there are immaterial features to human knowledge and freedom that denote the presence of an immaterial form or spiritual soul. There's also the whole architecture of virtue ethics Aquinas provides that is increasingly having an influence in the circles of analytical ethics. His study of the cardinal virtues—justice, prudence, temperance, and fortitude—provides terrific insight into the nature of a person. We're longing for that in a culture in which there's a great deal of intellectual instability and nostalgia for consensus. Often people want to impose consensus artificially through politics, which is a very superficial way to gain unity. That politics pervades the university, which is in crisis because there is deep absence of consensus about reality. Aquinas's general anthropology and moral theory can give us the basis for a much deeper agreement about what human beings are and the structure of moral life than can any identity politics.

Religion doesn't go away when you banish it from the university. It comes back in other forms, some of which are perfectly innocuous, but others of which are very dangerous. Aquinas is very realistic about the possibilities of pathological religious behavior; he calls it *superstitio,* the vice of disordered religion. The human being can become, very easily, irrationally religious, as, for example, in the cases of a banal religious emotivism or religiously motivated terrorism. The great conflicts we have between religionists and secularists, it seems to me, are very helpfully addressed by the harmony of reason and revelation in Aquinas, which allows the soul to flourish because the soul is meant for transcendence. Modern secular culture is asphyxiating. The soul needs to be open to the transcendent mystery of God to really experience the full freedom of its own intellectual life, its own voluntary life, its aspiration to the good, and its deepest desires for transcendence and meaning. A culture without an intellectual religious horizon is a truncated culture, but a culture that's religious at the expense of the intellectual life is also a very unhealthy culture—so how do you get that right? I think Aquinas really helps us understand our natural religious aspirations in a balanced way.

Which saints are you trying to conform to?

Perhaps we could speak of inspiration more than conformity. I'm a Dominican, so our great exemplar is Saint Dominic, who is in some ways a very hidden figure, historically speaking. St. Dominic sought to preach and live the Gospel in a deeply coherent way. He was a person of great Eucharistic and Marian devotion, who preached zealously and courageously but who also lived with his brothers in humility. In a certain way he hid himself amid the brethren as a humble man of God in regular prayer and common life. That's really beautiful. Every Dominican seeks to imitate Saint Dominic, very imperfectly in my case, but I think that's what we'd aspire to. Of course, there's Saint Thomas because he has this wonderfully constant, consistent search for the truth at the center of his preaching, teaching, writing, and love of souls. Saint Catherine of Sienna beautifully expresses what it means for the soul to be a bride of Christ and seek mystical union with God animated by the concerns of Christ. These people are wonderful exemplars for those of us in the Dominican Order. There's a lot of other saints who show us what God's grace is like in the life of a human person. In St. Teresa of Avila, Joan of Arc, the Cure D'Ars, or Charles de Foucauld, you see the mystery of Christ imprinting himself on a soul. Or Mother Theresa—what it is like when Christ impresses his own visage, his own face, onto the soul of that person so they become another Christ in the world. We could talk about others, but I think those figures are an immense consolation because they show the consistent reality of Christ present in the heart of the Church. Maybe not in a way that's quantitatively overwhelming but which is qualitatively so intensive as to manifest the fidelity of God to the Church in and through time.

Do you have further thoughts for those who may be early in their search for the truth?

The great enemy is intellectual despair. It's extremely important to persevere in seeking the truth with open horizons. We have to avoid being paralyzed by superficial intellectual conventions because convention sometimes stultifies people. Some cultural convention can be a safeguard in preserving what many people know to be true and sane. But in our life of seeking the truth, we have to transcend conformism, resist despair, and remain ardent in the search for the truth. The other thing is to find wise teachers. The idea that we can seek the truth all alone is foolish; we need wise teachers and friends, some who are dead and some who are living. A third and in fact related point: I have yet to meet someone who regretted becoming Catholic. I've talked to a lot of people who were very nervous about it before hand, very afraid, wondering if they were making a mistake. But it's like a doorway you have to step across. You're going to find peace and fulfillment, and will not regret it, but you have to take that step. The sacraments are an extremely powerful source of grace, and in a sense, this can only be discovered by experience. They work, *ex opere operato,* from the very work of the rite. When you begin to receive the sacraments regularly, you receive inward peace and resolution. When I was becoming Catholic, a Benedictine monk told me to go regularly to confession, every week or two, and to go to Mass often, every day if possible, and said that this would be the most helpful thing to do. I thought that sounded a little mechanical, but he knew the truth of the matter, which is that God works through the sacraments, so if you approach them with goodwill, they will change you over time.

It's not really that complicated. If you engage with God on God's terms according to the Church's teachings, God will sanctify you and you will achieve real friendship with God. That doesn't mean you won't suffer, but your suffering will take place in Christ, and that's deeply meaningful and consoling. The real answer is to enter the Catholic Church and live the sacramental life, and not despair in the search for the truth, because God is always very close to us and will give us the means to arrive at the destination if we want him to do so.

Chapter Six

"I Am Catholic Today as an Answer to Prayer"

Kirsten Powers

Interviewed by Kathryn Jean Lopez

Kirsten Powers is a columnist for *USA Today*, a CNN political analyst, and co-host of the podcast *The Faith Angle*. Previously a Fox News Channel commentator, she is author of *The Silencing* (Regnery). Powers wrote in 2013 about her conversion to Christianity in *Christianity Today* (which became their most read web story for the year) and contributed "The first Noel: Christmas with Jesus" to the book *The Christmas Virtues* (Templeton). A native of Alaska, she lives in Washington, DC.

Kathryn Jean Lopez is senior editor at the National Review Institute where she directs the Center for Religion, Culture, and Civil Society and is editor-at-large of *National Review* magazine. She's been at *NR* for over twenty years and was previously editor of *NR*'s website. She's a nationally syndicated columnist and contributor to many publications including *Angelus* from the Archdiocese of Los Angeles and fortnightly columnist at *OSV Newsweekly*. She's been published by the *Wall Street Journal* and the *New York Times* and appeared on CNN and Fox News among others, including EWTN. She was awarded the annual Washington Women in Journalism Award for Outstanding Journalism in the Periodic Press from CQ *Roll Call* in 2016 for writing about Christian genocide and persecution. Lopez serves on a number of boards and is a member of the Pro-Life Commission of the Archdiocese of New York, and speaks frequently on "first principle" issues including virtue, especially gratitude. She's co-author of *How to Defend the Faith without Raising Your Voice* (OSV) and a contributor to *When Women Pray* (Sophia), among other books. In 2012, Pope Benedict XVI presented her with a message for women throughout the world, as a representative of all the women of the world. A graduate of the Catholic University of America, she's also a certified spiritual director through the Cenacle of Our Lady of Divine Providence School of Spirituality and the Franciscan University of Steubenville, which focuses on Ignatius's approach to the spiritual life.

Kirsten Powers's maternal grandparents were "traditional Boston Catholics," as she describes them. "Faith was everything to them."

She doesn't doubt, either, that her conversion story has very much to do with sacramental grace. When her family started attending an Episcopal church in Alaska, her grandfather announced that the children were already baptized in a Catholic Church. Which, in retrospect, makes so much of her journey in faith as an adult make much more sense than it seemed to her along the way. Like when Fr. Jonathan Morris, a colleague on Fox News shows, announced "you know you are Catholic, right?"

The clincher moment on a long journey of crossing the Tiber happened not far from the river by that name in Rome, as it happens. Reluctant to at first, our mutual friend the late Kate O'Beirne—once described as the "crème de la crème of Washington insiderdom"—but more importantly a beloved and grateful daughter of God and fellow claustrophobic, talked Kirsten into going on the Scavi tour. Walking the catacombs under St. Peter's Basilica at the Vatican is the retelling of an adventure of faith and hope that ends with St. Peter's bones. At that moment, Kirsten was *ready*—all but insisting she become Catholic immediately, as the crowds at his funeral Mass once clamored in the square there for "sainthood now" for Pope John Paul II. She wanted, to use a JPII line, to become what she was.

I've known Kirsten since before she was a Christian—first meeting her when she was dating a mutual friend and colleague who was instrumental in her conversion. What I admire most about her is her transparency. She's an honest seeker of truth and is the first to admit that Truth himself has been seeking her for quite a long time. And so it continues. The best part of her conversion story is that when you sit down and talk to her about it, it is clear that it continues. We are not finished products, God continues to work on our transformation into him, if we allow him. Many of us fight. When I sat down with Kirsten for this interview, she exhibited the joy of one who has been sought and allows herself to be found by God. Not once but every day.

Kathryn Jean Lopez: *An observation: You have a beautiful trust and confidence in the power of prayer and in God's power to put you in situations and be with you. Do you feel that that's the case, that you have this regular trust, this gift of trust? Do you think it's a gift? And where did it come from?*

Kirsten Powers: I do ultimately believe that all. Of course, that doesn't mean that I don't sometimes forget it! I am human and I have my little periods of panic, but then I usually can reorient myself and remember that God's in control. And I want him to be! He has my best interests at heart, and so I will always ultimately end up back in a place of peace with him. I think the further I've gone along in my Christian walk, the faster that happens. There used to be more of a lag time. I'm now pretty quick to get myself there, and if I don't get myself there, a friend usually can get me there pretty quickly.

Where did this belief come from? I think I had it even before I was a believer, even when I went through atheist and agnostic periods. I grew up Episcopalian, but I didn't have any kind of real faith that was based on any kind of theology. Even so, I did have a faith in God, and I prayed to God, and I felt protected by God.

I only really remembered this after I became a Christian, but when I was about five—and this was before we ever went to church—I was somehow alone in the living room at my family's home. I think it may have been Billy Graham who was on the TV. He said: *If you want to receive Jesus, get down on your knees now, and ask him into your heart.* And so I don't know why I did it, no one had ever talked to me about this, but for some reason, I did it. In hindsight, I know what was behind it: God was always with me, even when I didn't technically believe. And so I always have had this trust. Even when I became sort of agnostic and atheist, I still had this kind of sense of being taken care of and watched out for that I couldn't really articulate.

And to be clear, that doesn't mean I think things are going to go my way, or that I'm going to get what I want, or that I'm always going to be safe, or that I'm always going to be healthy. It's just that God will be there. God will give me the grace to deal with the situation that is scary, or upsetting. When I became a Christian, I think that belief became theologically grounded in that this is what God promises us.

So how does somebody go from being Christian to agnostic to atheist to evangelical Christian to Catholic? How does that journey all work?

For one thing, I would say: I was never technically an evangelical, even though people have said that, probably because

I wrote my testimony about becoming Christian for *Christianity Today*, and I think they'd be pretty much considered an evangelical magazine. But I always describe myself as an "orthodox Christian," just meaning I believe the Bible's true; a more progressive Christian would say most of it's just metaphorical. I never identified as evangelical because I just think it's so weighted down with so many political overtones. When they believe me to be an evangelical, people would assume then I had become a right-wing Christian, which wasn't the case.

You know some of the story about how the man I was dating really wanted me to go to church with him. He had told me he couldn't marry someone who wasn't Christian. And it was in Tim Keller's church in Manhattan where I became a believer. Tim made the case that God is real and Christianity is true. It was the more compelling worldview. Later I had a powerful dream where I encountered Jesus. "Here I am," he said. It was so powerful; I couldn't shake it. I reached out to (bestselling evangelical writer and preacher) Eric Metaxas, who I had become friends with, and he suggested I start going to Kathy Keller's Bible study, and that was pretty much the rest of it. I was totally transformed. Everything changed.

And it was such a shock to my system. I went from living in a totally secular, atheist world and now I was in the evangelical world. Honestly, I wanted things to be the way they used to be. It was more comfortable there. But I couldn't get away from it. I felt like everywhere I turned, God was in my face. I couldn't deny that. And so I just kind of stuck with it, and then eventually kind of settled into: *Okay, I'm a believer.*

I'm so grateful to the Kellers. I also always felt like I wasn't totally connecting there. I'd read the Bible, but I felt like there was something more.

I moved from Redeemer (where Keller ministers) to Trinity Grace, which is a nondenominational evangelical church, and then I moved to DC, and I started going to an Anglican church. And that whole time I was just never settled.

Do you see God's hand in those steps of your journey?

Absolutely. If I had just become Catholic, straight in, I wouldn't even have been able to really make an informed decision. And so, yeah, so I was so grateful to them—Kathy and Tim are amazing, just brilliant. I met so many incredible people. But I always felt like a fish out of water. I always felt like: *This isn't me, I'm not a conservative, Republican, and I don't see the same, I don't understand all the emphasis of the things that they put emphasis on.* I was feeling alienated. And it got to the point where while church used to be the highlight of my week, it started to become a chore. I started going every other week, and I dreaded it.

And then around that time I started communicating a lot with people at the United States Conference of Catholic Bishops on different political issues, including poverty and immigration. God was opening another door.

Tell me about the Scavi. You're on a surprise pilgrimage to Rome and what happens?

It really was a surprise—all of it. Ann Corkery, who is now my godmother and a godmother of sorts to many in DC and beyond, and your beloved friend and colleague Kate O'Beirne, sprung the idea on me over a lunch. It's God's hand that I even said yes to lunch with them in the first place because I often don't make time for such things! But, of course, I wanted to be around Kate, everyone did. I have so much gratitude for both of them. Fast forward, though, to our pilgrimage to Rome. [Ann sponsors semi-annual trips for journalists to learn more about the Vatican and be spiritually energized.] Fr. Roger Landry, who ultimately got me ready and received me into the Church, stopped me in the hallway and asked, "Are you coming on the Scavi tour later?" I told him I simply couldn't. He insisted, "Kirsten, this may be the most important thing you ever do in your life." I was speechless. Because I couldn't do it. I couldn't handle it.

Kate must have overheard this and she approached me and explained she understood and wasn't going to go because she's been through it before and she's claustrophobic and was going to avoid that stress. "But it's really important," she said. "You should go, so I'll go with you." And then she totally lied to me and said, "And it's not that bad." When we walked in, too, and the door shut behind us and I started hyperventilating, she added, "This is the worst, it gets much better." Total lie.

[Kathryn and Kirsten laugh.]

I trust God has forgiven her.

Yes, especially since it totally calmed me down. She was just always right by my side and her presence calmed me down. And so we do the whole thing, and it's obviously very powerful to see how much these people believed, and to hear about how persecuted they were. And when we went in to where Peter's bones are buried, that just blew me away. Fr. Landry explained everything about how they figured out that they were Peter's bones, and they didn't know that they were Peter's bones, and how Jesus had said, "On this rock I will build my Church." And it was all just so incredibly real to me.

As I remember hearing about it from you and our friends at the time, you were ready.

I was, in many ways. But I also wanted to study, I wanted to do it right. So I came back to the United States, and I started reading. And I wish I had kept a journal and I wish I could remember all the books I read, because I read a lot. I know I read Scott Hahn. He was particularly help-ful because he had been an evangelical pastor, and he was able to go theologically through all of the objections. One of the things that I realized right away is just how much misinformation is out there about the Catholic Church, about what Catholics believe. He helped me through a lot of that: turns out Catholics don't worship Mary, and they don't worship saints!

Another book that helped me was *A Severe Mercy*, which my boyfriend who first got me to go to church gave me. I don't know why he gave it to me, but it had to be inspired, it was just such the right book for me. One of my struggles with Christianity was that I thought it was anti-intellectual. And, of course, that book is about professors at Oxford. My parents were professors and so that helped me a lot. I really thought all intellectuals were skeptics, so the book was the occasion for a major turning point for me, helping me let go of that caricature. And so I think that book, for me, was really meaningful and effective—for another person it might not be at all.

One of the things that affected me, too, was the idea that the Protestant Reformation was supposed to be just this brief period of reforming the Catholic Church. The whole idea was, yes, there were problems with the Catho-lic Church, and it needed to be reformed, and once there's reform we can all be one church again. We're all supposed to be united the way Jesus said. And near nobody is trying to do that in the Protestant world. We are supposed to be unified and that the Catholic Church is the true Church. The Catholic Church is the true Church, and so I'm obligated to be integrated into it. Once you see that, you are.

Do I remember correctly that EWTN played a role, too, in your story?

Oh, yes, it certainly did. I binge-watched the series *Coming Home!*

Kate was convinced that was just about the best commercial for the Catholic Church that exists!

It may be. I watched every possible episode because it addressed all my theological questions. There was the atheist who became Catholic, the evangelical who became Catholic, the lapsed Catholic who came back, there was a scientist. . . . Oh, I watched so many of those! I listened to *Catholic Answers* too. I was talking with Fr. Landry and going to New York from Washington over a number of months, and having long talks with Ann. And at the same time, I was worried about what my evangelical friends were going to think.

What did they say?

That's funny, because while I expected them to freak out, the way it really played out is that they said, "Of course you're becoming Catholic. It's so obvious. You're so obviously Catholic. It totally makes sense."

And you seem so at home?

I love being Catholic. I love confession. It's so healthy. I love the idea of being able to go to Communion whenever I want—as long as I've been to confession. It all feels to me like: *this is what it's supposed to be like.* If faith is the most important thing in your life, you should be at Mass regularly. It's strange that so many churches only have a service on Sundays. The Catholic Church is taking Christianity seriously. There is so much wisdom in the Catholic Church. And I noticed so much healthy human interaction, too, immediately. Whereas some evangelicals struggle with men and women being alone in a room together, especially if we're talking about the pastor, I can talk to my Dominican priest friends without being made to feel like a walking temptation. I can see the wisdom in celibacy for the kingdom, where it makes for a unique availability for God. It was all such a totally different experience of life and faith when I became Catholic.

And, honestly, I just decided it was true. That's the bottom line. This is true. I had been dragging my feet for human reasons—especially because of a fear of what my evangelical friends would say. But then one night I was sitting on my sofa, and *Coming Home,* of course, was on. And someone quotes a pope saying that once you become aware that the Catholic Church is the one true Church and you don't convert, you're putting your salvation in jeopardy. I immediately bolted up. I literally texted Father Landry asking, "Is this true?" He said yes—that if you see it as true, in good conscience you have to make a move. And that was it for me. I told him I have to do this now, we need to do this like, yesterday. The rest is, as they say, history.

I remember what looked and sounded like tremendous joy when you became Catholic, even as you announced it on The Five on

Fox News and over Twitter that night, but also in our conversations. Where does that come from? How do you explain that?

It was the most joyful experience of my life! It really was just absolute joy. My friend Kelly observed this too, saying how different I was. It was the graces of the sacraments. It's real. I was just so happy. And every day I seemed to be opening new gifts. I would discover another box to open and learn about. Even now I'm now getting into early Catholic mysticism and all the teachings of contemplatives are transforming my spiritual life. There is so much to know and learn! There are so many amazing saints. I've never heard of so many of these people! The Church fathers were new to me. So many of the nuns, past and present, were new to me. There's so much history; there are so many treasures.

One of the treasures you've mentioned to me over time is the women you discovered in the Church. I know you love your Confirmation saint, Edith Stein. What is it about the Catholic Church and women you love?

Oh, I love Edith Stein! I think I discovered her one day while browsing at the bookstore by the shrine [The Basilica of the National Shrine of the Immaculate Conception by the Catholic University of America].

One of the first things I noticed when I started reading more seriously about the Catholic Church is the women. I'd discover saint so-and-so was a doctor of the Church. She advised popes, and at a young age. I couldn't believe this was all news to me. I discovered this tremendous reverence that existed for these women. And as thinkers. For me, someone who is not a mother, this was just so beautiful to discover.

I love Teresa of Avila and want to read more.

I remember on *Coming Home*, hearing men talk about how a particular saint helped them into the Church. I found this amazing. This is not something I was used to hearing from Christians. And it's not just the saints. I love Dorothy Day, for instance.

What about Mary?

She was not an obstacle for me. I was so happy that there was a woman so central to the Faith. Look, I consider myself a feminist, so this makes me happy, but it's about more than that. It just makes sense. You can't have life without the feminine, so of course we would be central to the Christian story.

And you love Pope Francis?

I do. He wasn't what drew me to Catholicism. I always really liked Pope Benedict. I read his books on Jesus and they helped me and I already had an affection for the Catholic Church, but I like fell head over heels in love with Francis from the word "go." He wasn't the reason I became Catholic, but I think he was like the cherry on top. I just felt like I was looking at Jesus. I just felt like: *Wow, this is a person that just really walks the walk, in a way that people can see.*

Also, one of the things also that I loved about Pope Francis is how the media couldn't get enough of him from the beginning. We hear so much about the "nones"—people who are spiritual and not religious. And yet here they are drawn like a magnet to him. There's obviously a hunger. The Catholic Church matters in a way that I don't see other moral and religious leaders mattering. Remember how he was covered when he came here to the US? This is not how a person people don't care about gets treated. They were talking about him! It gave me so much hope. He was drawing people home and the media was covering it! People talk about the controversial things, but there are beautiful things we need to talk about more. We let things get so politicized and it hurts hungry people in the process. Let's talk not about women priests but the value of women which the Catholic Church is a herald of!

What about disagreements? What about issues where you're not quite sure you agree with where the Church comes down?

Here's my experience of the Church: Overall what I've seen is women being taken pretty seriously, I feel like I've been taken seriously, and there are a lot of women academics who are taken very seriously. Also, it always comes back to: What do I think is true? I believe the Catholic Church is true, so I accept her teachings. It's an institution made up of human beings and there will be sin and failings. Which is why we must pray for the pope and everyone else. We're all people in the end, after all. We need to pray for the guidance of the Holy Spirit always, for all of us. I think we have to have a lot of humility and want to grow in spiritual maturity.

But you had some struggle, too, soon after, didn't you, after being received into the Church?

A crisis! So, I became Catholic, and not that soon after was the synod on the family in Rome and so all of the sudden I see all this fighting between conservative Catholics and progressive Catholics, or liberal Catholics, or whatever they are being called. I immediately thought: *This is totally what I was trying to get away from.* I could not believe what was going on and how mean people are being to Pope Francis, frankly. It was upsetting. So I immediately started not feeling at home, wondering if I belonged here after all. I wanted to be Catholic. I didn't want to have to be categorized as a Republican Catholic or a Democratic Catholic. I want my faith to inform everything else. I can't relate to people who are overtly in any political camp. Look, I'm typically a left-center person, but I have views that are considered conservative as well. I want to follow my faith. I don't want to be put in a political box. Ideology can be a dangerous thing—and jeopardize your faith. It can close you off to the Holy Spirit, the will of God for you. It's a struggle when I see people—Christians—and how badly they behave on social media. We have to be better.

Do you feel different as a commentator now that you're Christian? Do you feel like since people know you are Catholic, you better be living to a higher standard even as you are talking about politics? Do you find yourself debating and engaging differently than you once did?

Yes. I think about it especially when I screw up.

How so? By way of an examination of conscience?

Yes. I think about it most when I don't do well. It's when I realize I was dismissive or raised my voice, wasn't respectful. I realize I really wish I hadn't done that. It's not right and I'm pretty publicly known as Christian and that's not how Christians behave. I almost always go and ask for forgiveness from the person I did it to.

And it can be easy in those circumstances—in the busy-ness of the green room—to be dismissive, even to ignore the makeup person, because you're thinking about what you have to say.

Yes. Or when you're in a heated argument, or somebody's just saying something over and over that's not true, and they're talking over you, and interrupting you . . . human nature kicks in. People ask me, "How do you stay so calm with all this craziness about you?" The answer is: I pray—a ton. I think people think I'm joking when I say it, but I'm not. I'm a human like anybody else that has the capacity to get angry and really affected by these things. Prayer makes the difference, and gives me kind of a perspective.

Do people ask you about your faith a lot because you're open about it?

A little bit, yeah. It's funny, the other day I had a friend of mine from high school who I hadn't talked to in a long time. We follow each other on Instagram, and I'd been posting about books that I'm reading, mostly Catholic books. And so she told me that she's been thinking about going back to church for a while and shared that she went the other day, and just didn't feel any connection. She knew I had converted and she wanted to talk. And so we're going to FaceTime, and I'm going to talk to her. This kind of conversation is becoming more regular, especially from people who have fallen away from the Faith. If I can help them in any way, I'm grateful. I just love that.

What do you think about when you look at Jesus on the cross?

I think about how my identity was stripped away when I first became Christian and how that's an ongoing process still. I really felt so out of place; like I told you earlier, it was a total shock to my system, to everything I knew and was comfortable with. It would have been a lot easier to stay where I was. But I'm grateful to God and I'm grateful for the process. I'm grateful to everyone who helped along the way. It's all helped me have a real empathy for people who feel alone, who don't feel like they fit in. Prayer helps so much. Even when I feel drawn away, he pulls me back. It's not always enjoyable, but it's the Holy Spirit at work. I consent. And he focuses me. It keeps changing everything. Relationships, everything. The fruits of faith and prayer are undeniable.

Chapter Seven

Slapped Across the Face
by the Church Fathers

Joshua Charles

Interviewed by Sherif Girgis

Joshua Charles is an historian, writer, and speaker. He has authored and co-authored bestselling books on America's founders, Israel, and the Bible. A concert pianist with an MA in government and a law degree, Joshua has performed and spoken around the world. His writing has been featured in numerous publications, including *Fox News*, *The Federalist*, and the *Jerusalem Post*, among others. He has served several organizations, including the Museum of the Bible, the American Bible Society, the Jerusalem Institute of Justice. After a lifetime spent as a born and raised Protestant, Joshua decided to become Catholic after spending nearly a year reading the Church Fathers, and more than 260 other books on the Catholic faith.

Sherif Girgis, a PhD student in philosophy at Princeton and a Catholic convert from (lapsed) Coptic Orthodoxy, has written and spoken widely in academic and popular venues on moral, religious, and social issues. A 2008 graduate of Princeton, *summa cum laude*, he earned a JD from Yale and a BPhil (MPhil) in philosophy from Oxford as a Rhodes Scholar.

Sherif Girgis: *What was your religious experience growing up? Were there Catholics among your relatives and friends? What did you believe about (and think of) the Catholic Church?*

Joshua Charles: I was raised as, essentially, a non-denominational Protestant Christian. We attended services at churches that seemed to take the Bible seriously and adhered to a modicum of Christian orthodoxy on theological and moral matters. I had several Catholic relatives, but they were nominal, and Catholicism never came up. I was never interested, and they never told me about it. We attended a few Catholic Masses with these relatives when I was younger, but that was the extent of my exposure to the Church. As with most services when I was a kid, I tried to sleep as much as possible.

Years ago you began having doubts about the doctrine of sola scriptura ("Scripture alone"). What prompted those doubts, and what did you conclude at the time? Do you remember why you weren't then prompted to consider Catholicism or Orthodoxy?

My doubts about *sola scriptura* have been present for many years, but only around 2015 did I officially reject the doctrine (though I kept that fact private). I have always loved the Bible and studied it very carefully. I basically conceived the problem this way: There are, in the Scripture itself, always two voices of authority: the authority of the Scripture and a living authority, whether in the guise of Moses, the Judges of Israel, the priests, the prophets, King David and Solomon, and then finally Jesus and the Apostles. These stood side by side—Scripture and Living Authority—throughout the Bible.

Next I considered the question while traversing chronologically through the Bible. For example, if I was a first-century peasant and Jesus was speaking to me, was what he was saying authoritative? Of course. He's the Messiah. But that means something outside of Scripture is fully authoritative. Moving forward, let's say I was hearing the Apostles preach outside the Temple in Acts. Is what they are saying to me authoritative? Again, of course, because they are the Apostles. Once again, something *outside* the Scripture had full, divinely given authority. That gets us to the Council of Jerusalem in Acts 15. This council delivered a *dogma* (the actual Greek word), and Acts 16 makes clear that this dogma was delivered to all the Church *for their observance*. In other words, this council had defined an authoritative rule of faith and morals related to the relationship between Jews and Gentiles, and the churches were expected to *obey* it. Thus, we continue to have, in the Bible itself, the authority of Scripture alongside a Living Authority, invested with divine prerogative.

The Council of Jerusalem is even more interesting because of who was part of it, and the role Scripture played. I always had excused the council as an argument against *sola scriptura* by saying that it was made up of the Apostles, and thus would of course have divine authority. But that isn't true. It was made up of the Apostles *and the elders* (i.e., non-Apostles). Thus, non-Apostles, already in the very first few decades of the Church, are themselves somehow invested with binding, divine authority. Next, when James cites Scripture toward the end of Acts 15, he cites the book of Amos, and the verses he quotes have absolutely *nothing* to do with what sorts of foods Gentiles may eat, and which portions of the Torah they must obey (which was what the council was deciding). The verses were, *thematically*, about the calling of the Gentiles. But as far as the content, it was not at all "on point" to the specific issue of kosher laws, or any other matter directly dealt with by the council. Indeed, the council itself, in its letter, says, "For it has seemed good *to the Holy Spirit and to us* to lay on you no greater burden than these requirements." What is mentioned is the Holy Spirit, and the Church—there is no mention of Scripture. Does that *downgrade* Scripture? Absolutely not. But it clearly exhibits the reality of divinely invested authority that is outside of it.

This was the breaking point for me—seeing that the Scripture itself never once exhibits the idea of *sola scriptura* in practice. This was additionally confirmed by the fact that the Scripture itself *never* says when this living voice of authority ceased. If it did, I could perhaps believe in *sola scriptura*. But it doesn't. So for the first time in my life, Jesus's delegation of authority to "bind and loose" and to forgive sins began making sense—but only within the context of a *Living, authoritative voice of authority in the Church*, guided by the Holy Spirit.

I would also ask many of my friends this question: "The letter the Council of Jerusalem sent to the churches, outlining what they must do: did that have authority *when written*, or only after it was included in the Bible?" This was the stump question. If it didn't have authority, then the council was remarkably presumptuous, and essentially committed sacrilege by appealing to the authority of the Holy Spirit, as well as their own, for what they were doing. But if it *did* have authority, then that meant that, once again, there was an authority outside of the Bible itself that was divinely ordained and binding on Christians. And the Bible *never* says that this Living Authority ended. In fact, many of Paul's epistles are full of exhortations to obey the very men that were appointed by him, or by the overseers he had appointed, because of their God-given authority.

Thus, it is no exaggeration to say that a close and careful reading of the Bible itself eviscerated the idea of *sola scriptura* in my mind. But the issue of the canon (i.e., the list of books that are divinely inspired, which the Bible itself never provides) also played a role. The Church does not create the canon, but it does recognize it. But if I adhered to *sola scriptura*, which says that the Bible is the sole *infallible* authority in the Church, then the idea of an infallible canon was simply no longer coherent, because by necessity, one would have to appeal to things outside of the Bible for the contents of that canon, as the Bible never defines it, either in the Old or New Testaments. So the final question was: *whom* do I trust to get that canon correct? Who is the divinely ordained authority by which we may be certain that we have the correct canon? Myself? Scholars at universities? The Jesus Seminar? I concluded that my appeal must be to nothing more and nothing less than the authority we see exhibited throughout the Scripture, but particularly in Acts 15, and that is the Living, Authoritative Church that began at Pentecost, and who, despite all her flaws, is the recipient of a divinely-vouched promise from Christ himself, that the gates of hell would *never* prevail against her.

Did you have other experiences or insights (before last year) that you now see as having set you on this path?

Yes. I had to consider this idea: is Christianity something I make up for myself, or is it something that is handed on to me? Because everywhere I look, Christianity in America seems in chaos. There are many holy, righteous Christians. But there is disagreement on just about everything. Growing up in the Protestant world, I was constantly told that differences over baptism, the sacraments, communion, church government, pastoral authority, marriage and divorce, and a whole host of moral issues were simply "differences between brothers." Beyond the barebones of the Trinity and the salvific work of Christ, the only thing that all Protestants seemed to be absolutely certain about was "we aren't Catholic." Thus, they could disagree about many of the aforementioned issues, but one of their key points of certainty was a mere negation. I found this deeply dissatisfying. From the time I was young, though I never really pursued the question, I was always disturbed by the idea that the Church got it wrong for fifteen hundred years (i.e., the vast majority of its history), but only five hundred years ago, we suddenly got it right. But once we did, apparently, get it right, we began disagreeing on just about everything. This was, in my mind, an incoherency at the heart of Protestantism that only grew the older I got—no doubt exacerbated by my increasing vexation with American Evangelicalism.

The most deliberate leg of your journey began with intense reading of the Church Fathers about a year ago. What prompted you to read them? Whom did you read? How did you structure your reading? Which works or lines of argument or pieces of evidence did you find especially convincing?

I had seen a thirty-eight-volume set of the writings of the Church Fathers for many years, going back to my college days. Being a bibliophile, I'm particularly attracted to multi-volume sets, and I've always loved history. Thus, for many years, I knew I wanted to get this set. But it was expensive—over a month's worth of rent in my college days—and I simply couldn't afford it.

Then I got to law school and was also working full-time making a good income, and I could easily afford it, but I was living in Virginia and knew I'd be moving back home to California soon. So I decided to wait. I already knew I'd be moving about two thousand books three thousand miles across the country, so I didn't want to add to that burden.

So I finally arrived back home in California in May of 2017. I decided to treat myself for graduating law school, and I purchased the set of the Church Fathers' writings I had had my eyes on for probably five to six years. Catholicism was *not* on my mind. I wasn't looking for it. All I knew was I was extremely dissatisfied with "church" as I knew it. My faith was strong as ever, but I simply didn't know what to do as far as church was concerned. Ironically, in the previous month (April), I had posted on my Facebook "I do not believe that history means everything, so I *can't be a Catholic*. On the other hand, I don't believe history means nothing, and therefore I can't be a full Protestant either. An interesting conundrum to be in." [Emphasis added]

Then, in early June, the set arrived. I opened the first volume—the Apostolic Fathers. I began reading the words of Clement of Rome, of Ignatius of Antioch, of Justin Martyr, and Irenaeus of Lyons, and I was absolutely slapped across the face. These men were talking about the Real Presence of Christ in the Eucharist, the Eucharist as a sacrifice, the authority of bishops, the authority of the church of Rome, tradition alongside Scripture, the unity of the Church, apostolic succession, and even citing what I had been taught were "apocryphal" books as Scripture.

It is difficult to describe how much of a shock this was. I had had some private discussions with some Protestant friends, and all of them could only tell me "they are just men," and therefore just because they interpreted the Bible in a certain way didn't necessarily make them right. But this response was deeply unsatisfying. After all, the Apostles were just men—Luke was just a man—all the prophets and judges and kings of Israel were just men. Not only that, but these men were much closer to the origins of the Faith, and some had even been discipled by the Apostles themselves. Could I afford to so casually ignore them?

So by the end of June, I had posted on my Facebook as follows: "Why, I wonder, are there some who insist that reading the writings of those Church Fathers who both knew and were discipled by the Apostles (or their disciples) is somehow less reliable than reading Martin Luther, John Calvin, and the like, who lived 1,500 years later? Who would common sense dictate is more trustworthy in their doctrine? I leave this to the unprejudiced mind to determine." The transformation had begun. And I was getting very, *very* nervous. While I denied it at the time, inwardly I could see what was coming on the horizon; I could see that for the first time I was considering what, my whole life, I had been taught should be *unconsidered*. I could sense my entire life was quite possibly on the brink of a profound change. And it made me fearful.

But I continued. I went on to purchase over 250 books on Catholicism. I re-read and re-watched many of the books, sermons, and debates from many of the voices I had listened to for years—the John MacArthurs, the R. C. Sprouls, the Wayne Grudems. To this day, I deeply respect these men. But I could no longer ignore how their vision of the truth was completely contradicted by the Church Fathers I was reading on a daily basis.

How did your reading of the Church Fathers begin shaping your prayer, worship, and reading of the Scriptures? Were there insights or disciplines that you think even non-Catholic Christians can and should avail themselves of to draw closer to Christ?

There is an immense amount of admiration that *all* Christians can have for the Church Fathers, and much they say that speaks to *all* Christians. The reason the Church Fathers turned out to be such a crucial turning point for me was because of the absence of any *distinctively* Protestant doctrines among their writings, and the presence of a great deal of *distinctively* Catholic doctrines. Many of them were martyred, so studying their lives is a must. Much of this can be done directly from their writings. Fathers like Athanasius were incredibly brave and faced physical threats to life and limb quite often. Ambrose stood up to the Roman emperor Theodosius, and the emperor ended up repenting of some barbarous acts and doing penance. Polycarp faced a horrific death at the hands of pagan Romans. Justin Martyr has his name for a reason. Ignatius of Antioch wrote brilliant letters to the churches along his path from Antioch to Rome, on his way to a martyr's death. These men were brilliant, articulate, and courageous. And while the doctrines and ideas they discuss tend to be far closer to Catholicism, there is nonetheless a great deal that *all* Christians can appreciate—in the same way that Protestants still share a good deal in common with Catholics to this day.

What other materials did you consult? Were there people—Catholics or otherwise—whose advice you found especially helpful?

I had many resources at my disposal. Most were books, but I also watched a ton of convert interviews and Catholic apologetic material online. Scott Hahn was a huge influence, as was Bishop Robert Barron. The wit and wisdom of G. K. Chesterton were influential, as was the quiet wisdom of J. R. R. Tolkien (the Catholic who played an important role in the conversion of C. S. Lewis to Christianity). I also read a good deal of official Church documents and saw an immensely impressive work of deeply coherent theology and morality. Joseph Cardinal Ratzinger/Pope Benedict XVI wrote a number of works I found insightful. I was also impressed by the case for Catholicism made by Francis de Sales. Ironically, reading the writings of the Reformers themselves made me more attracted to Catholicism. I had read a good deal of them for many years, but after reading the Church Fathers, and re-reading large portions of their writings, and thinking through it all with different presuppositions, I found their ideas wanting.

How have your family, friends, and colleagues reacted? Did any of their reactions make your decision harder? How have you tempered any strain on relationships?

Most people have responded positively. I was always the most "theological" in my family, and some of them have even fallen away from the Faith. If anything, they have been very intrigued. The same has been true of many of my friends, although some have very strong disagreements with me. However, when the issue has come up, they have often found themselves unable to answer some of the prime questions I was dealing with, and this has encouraged a more active dialogue. I do have some friends, however, who have essentially stopped communicating with me. That has been very sad for me. But I trust that in God's good timing, we shall reunite. And even if we don't, finding the Church has been entirely worth it. I had arrived at a point where I saw the Church as the "pearl of great price" for which we are enjoined to sell all. The sacrifices of many of the saints make my own "sacrifices" in this regard seem puny. If I let relational loss prevent me from doing what I knew to be true, just, and right, I would be utterly unworthy.

During your year of intense study of the Church Fathers, you used social media to keep people apprised of your thinking. Any striking or telling responses?

Yes. Many of my Protestant friends tried to dismiss them as "just men," and act as if their opinion should have no more bearing than that of any other "pastor" of today. I found this approach utterly nonsensical. How could I take the words of Ignatius, who was discipled by the Apostle John, or Clement of Rome, who is mentioned in the Bible, as seriously as some megachurch pastor, or some Protestant theologian thousands of years after the fact? To put those types of sources on the same level struck me then, and strikes me now, as a willful ignoring of truth and common sense. One issue in particular exemplifies the ruinous tendencies of this approach: prior to the Protestant "reformation," *every single Church Father* believed in baptismal regeneration. It was a *universal* Christian belief. The Church Fathers, like we do today, debated various issues, and disagreed amongst themselves, and with current Church teaching, on various issues (which illustrates the need for a Magisterium, by the way). But on issues like baptismal regeneration, there was *zero* disagreement. But then, I am confidently told by my Protestant brethren that baptismal regeneration is "clearly" unbiblical (I heard this often). My retort, often in the context of a social media post which quoted a Church Father speaking clearly on the reality of baptismal regeneration, was, "Well then why did all the Church Fathers, East and West, Greek and Latin, believe it was for nearly one thousand years, and Catholicism and Orthodoxy maintained that belief until the sixteenth century?" I got no response to this basic question. The reason why, in my view, is that it exposes Protestant pretensions for what they are. I don't mean that to refer to individual Protestants, but Protestant-*ism*. I know many holy, righteous, dear Protestants. They taught me the rudiments of the faith, and they taught me to love Jesus Christ and the Bible. But on issue after issue, many Protestants simply do not realize how aberrant Prot-estant*ism* is when viewed in light of the two-thousand-year history of Christianity. And the aberrations only continue to get worse after a mere five hundred years, whereas I can read my Catechism, and it aligns incredibly well with so much of what I read from the Church Fathers, as well as subsequent developments in the medieval and renaissance Church.

You helped develop the Global Impact Bible and have done im-portant work for the Faith & Liberty Discovery Center and for the Museum of the Bible in addition to lecturing around the world. Much of that work has involved compiling, sorting, and distilling vast quantities of historical material. Did any of that work have an impact on your journey? Are there specific ways you expect Catholicism to shape your future public work?

Yes. Years ago I began studying the Founding Fathers *ad fontes*—by going to the sources themselves. I was shocked to find tons of material I was never taught, and my love and respect for the Founders grew immensely. This approach was no doubt key to my conversion to Catholicism, as reading the Church Fathers was the key turning point for me. I had to ask myself: *Can I continue going along with my previous beliefs when so many of my Christian ancestors forcefully contradicted them?* Did I have the power to "veto" so much history, so much theology, so many decrees of councils just because of my own "right" to a personal opinion? I decid-ed that I did not. But this conviction was already present when it came to the Founders, and modern attempts by both "Right" and "Left" to manipulate them (usually out of ignorance) for their own purposes. A return to the sources, an *ad fontes* approach, which had been my approach in so much of my historical study and writing, is what ultimately brought me to the Church.

As far as Catholicism's effect on my future public work— no doubt. My beliefs are what the Magisterium teaches. End of story. I have been discouraged by the number of Catholics in the West who presume to take a cafeteria approach to the Magisterium. In my mind, this essentially makes them Catholics in name only. To pick and choose is what Protestants do (and one can see shards of Catholicism all over Protestantism—each sect and/or denomination takes some Catholic idea or doctrine and then changes it to its own liking). Either one accepts the teachings of the Church, or one doesn't. If you do, you are a faithful Catholic. If you don't, you are Catholic nominally, but functionally you are a Protestant. I intend to spend the rest of my life standing up for the Church, and the Judeo-Christian heritage of the West it was so involved in forming. We in the West desperately need a recovery of this heritage. Given current trends, Christianity will be saved by Asia and Africa. The West is quickly collapsing into its own now-vacuous soul. I believe the Church, if there is any cultural revival in the West whatsoever, will be essential to that revival. Catholicism is truly the religion "of our fathers." Let us return to the ancient paths and landmarks. Let us there rediscover ourselves.

Suppose someone wanted to get a snapshot of the sorts of evidence that changed your mind—but in fewer than four thousand pages! What handful of primary or secondary resources would you recommend to them?

Clement of Rome *Epistle to the Corinthians*; the *Epistles* of Ignatius of Antioch; various portions of Irenaeus's *Against Heresies*; the *Commonitory* of Vincent of Lerins; Francis de Sales *The Catholic Controversy*, et cetera. And quite frankly, my conversion was somewhat precipitated by a more thorough reading of Luther and Calvin. The more I read them, the more I came to see how erroneous the basis of their "doctrines" were. For example, reading of their direct appeal to the "inward illumination of the Holy Spirit" to change the canon of Scripture was a huge turning point for me. Calvin directly appeals to this, as does the Westminster Confession (based on his doctrines) about a century later. This appeal to some sort of inward and individualized illumination of the Holy Spirit I found to be an extremely precarious foundation upon which to define something as fundamental as the canon. The discovery that Luther and Calvin, in particular, were actually very *opposed* to the interpretation of the Bible by lay people was also a big revelation for me. Finally, realizing two facts was also key: the intense disagreement about fundamental issues among the earliest Protestant "reformers" themselves (according to which many Protestants today, according to Luther, Calvin, or Zwingli, would be heretics) as well as the way in which so many modern Protestants simply no longer believe anything approaching what their Protestant forebears believed and taught. Catholic doctrine has developed and been refined over time, no doubt. But it remains fundamentally the same on issue after issue after issue. The same cannot be said of the vast majority of Protestant denominations, which now number in the thousands.

Which spiritual writers have you found especially helpful? Are there particular forms of prayer or other ascetical practices that you would recommend to those committed to the life of the mind or to work as public intellectuals?

I'm still new to this. But I have been inspired by countless Catholic writers and saints, including the Church Fathers, Aquinas, Teresa of Avila, Francis of Assisi, Ignatius of Loyola, et cetera. More modern writers like G. K. Chesterton, Hilaire Belloc, Christopher Dawson, and Peter Kreeft are also great heroes of mine.

For many years, I have found the practice of fasting beneficial. I typically went for two to three days with only water and coffee/tea. It provided an opportunity to experience the reality that "man shall not live by bread alone, but by the Word of God," and spend more time in the Scriptures and in prayer. As a young man, I would be lying if I said I didn't continue to struggle with lust. I have found great solace in the writings of Saint Augustine and appealing to him for his intercession. There also key points in this whole conversion process where I appealed to the Blessed Mother to pray for guidance, and on many occasions, that was followed within less than twenty-four hours by some providential event. For example, in about October 2017, I sensed I was really stumbling onto something of life-changing proportions. I requested of the Blessed Mother that, if the Catholic Church really was Christ's Church, she would pray that I find even deeper confirmation of this. Literally the next day, I was exposed to the *Commonitory* of St. Vincent of Lerins. Written around AD 434, it was an absolutely breathtaking work. It had popes; Scripture and Tradition; an excoriation of *sola scriptura*, by which many heretics teaching very weird things (which many Protestants themselves would reject) had come up with their novel doctrines; an affirmation of the authority of the Church; et cetera. It absolutely blew me away.

I'm a big fan of "practicing the presence of God" as Brother Lawrence discusses. I do have times of the day when I purposely pray in a more formal way. But I'm also praying throughout the day. I'm surrendering (trying to at least) my vices to God and requesting the intercession of the saints, as well as Christ himself, for ever greater portions of the Divine Life in my soul and the courage to act on it.

Are there particular misconceptions about Catholicism that you were able to dispel for non-Catholic friends?

Yes. In short, one of the biggest reasons I never considered Catholicism prior to reading the Church Fathers is that I didn't understand it. I *thought* I did. But as Mark Twain supposedly said, what I "knew" just wasn't so. Whether it was the canon, the infallibility of the pope, indulgences, sacred tradition, the communion of saints, or Mary (a very big one for Protestants), I realized I had simply put Catholicism into a bunch of propagandistically-formed Protestant boxes that did not even come close to doing justice to actual Catholic teaching. That didn't automatically make the Church correct, but it did mean that my understanding was deeply problematic, as is that of most Protestants.

I also began to realize that, in technological terms, Catholics and Protestants have very different "software." So you can discuss one particular topic, but in reality, it is not so much disagreements on a series of individual topics that are the problem, but rather a very different set of assumptions and worldview foundations that Catholics and Protestants bring to the table.

Perhaps the biggest one, for me, was realizing that much of what Protestants consider an either/or, Catholics believe is a both/and. The most obvious example of this is faith and works. Many Protestants belief in *sola fide*, or "faith alone," to describe how we are saved. They say works are the *fruit* of an authentic faith, but do not play a role in saving us. Catholics say *prima fide*, or "faith first," and works are part and parcel of divinely-endowed charity aroused in the heart, and thus *do* play a role in our ultimate salvation, but that it's all a fruit of God—even our works are part of God's gift to us.

The same also applies to the broader Protestant schema of salvation. For most Protestants, you are "saved" at a particular point in time, and remain saved until you die, and then go to heaven (not all Protestants believe this, and this isn't doing full justice to the view, but that's the essence of it). For such Protestants, salvation is either something we can know *now* or can't know for sure. Catholics see this, once again, as a both/and. Catholics believe we are "saved" in the sense of being partakers of the divine life in the sacraments, but that none of us can presume that we will ultimately be "saved" unless we persevere in the Faith, as Scripture constantly enjoins.

This gets into a very important philosophical idea called the non-competitive principle. Protestants oftentimes believe that if we honor or venerate Mary, or a saint, or the pope, et cetera, that we are by default taking glory away from the only place it properly belongs; namely, Christ. But a Catholic doesn't see these things in competition. The Catholic reads the Bible where Jesus says that what we do to the least of these we do *to him*, and that loving others as we love ourselves is alongside the command to love God with all our heart, soul, mind, and strength. Thus, the Catholic believes that showing love to certain human beings is not taking glory *away* from Christ but is in fact giving glory to him—we honor and love God when we honor and love his servants. We honor and love God when we love others as ourselves. This should not be surprising, given that Christianity itself is based on the Incarnation—the mystical union of man and God in the person of Jesus Christ, with no diminishing of either.

I have often asked my married Protestant friends, "You love your wife/husband very much, don't you?" "Yes, of course I do." "And Christ commands you [husbands] to love your wife as Christ loves the Church, yes?" "Of course." "So if you show extravagant, sacrificial, never-ending love to your wife, are you taking anything away from Christ?"

That last question is often met with either an "Of course not!" or a blank stare. If they admit "Of course not," then they have already shown their understanding of the non-competitive principle. The blank stare usually means they know the Catholic has a point. These things are *not* in competition with each other, nor is God in competition with his creation. They are part and parcel of the same thing. The very Trinity itself exemplifies this—the Son receiving glory doesn't take away from the Father or the Spirit, and so on. Why do we venerate Mary? Because she leads us to Christ. Why do we venerate saints? Because they lead us to Christ. Throughout the Bible, God delegates divine authority to patriarchs, legislators, prophets, judges, kings, and Apostles. A God who does such a thing moves and breaths and acts through human agency. He sees it as no affront to his own prerogatives. It is, in fact, an expression of his prerogative to involve humans at all. And yet that's precisely what he does.

Perhaps the most stereotypical issue is the supposed dichotomy of faith and works. The way I have explained the Catholic view to Protestant friends is from the fourth chapter of the book of Revelation. We are in the throne room of heaven, and there are twenty-four elders seated on thrones, clothed in white garments, and wearing crowns of gold. All of these were given to them by God. And yet what do they do? They cast their crowns at the feet of God, as he alone who is worthy. And indeed he is, for God is *he alone* who is worthy *in and of himself*—by virtue of his very *being*. In this sense, all our works and merits, while truly ours, and truly meritorious, are merely *derivative*, as they are not part of the essence of our being. That's what makes grace so necessary. God's grace has given us what we need, the power of spirit, mind, and sound discipline, as Paul says. Thus, what we do with God's good gifts matters.

A more practical example I've used with my Protestant friends is this: Let's say someone is on top of a house in the aftermath of a hurricane. Everywhere is flooded, and waters are rushing around them, preventing them from being saved. But a Coast Guard helicopter arrives and someone on it extends a hand in order to save them. The trapped refugee grabs the hand and is saved. And I ask this question: what person in their right mind would *ever* give ultimate credit to the refugee for grabbing the hand that has been extended to him? That is nonsense. We give credit to the Coast Guard. *They* are ultimately responsible for the saving of that refugee.

The same is true of God and us, in the Catholic view. Jesus gives us talents (i.e., divine grace, *not* of ourselves, but wrought by the Spirit of God in the sacraments). And as he so clearly teaches, and as Scripture so clearly teaches, we are not only going to be held accountable for how we use those talents but whether we are "ready" when the Master returns. That is Catholic teaching. It's a both/and, not an either/or.

To summarize this view in one verse, I would, as Bishop Robert Barron does, point to Isaiah 26:12: "Lord, you will decree peace for us, for you have accomplished all we have done."

We *really* have done our good works. But it is the Lord's grace which has empowered us to do so, and thus the ultimate glory, merit, and honor, is his. We really have done it. But even then, it is him working in us. "Christ in us, the hope of glory," as the Apostle Paul says.

In short, what I thought I knew about Catholicism just wasn't true. I realized that the Catholic intellectual tradition is extremely powerful, and I studied what the Church actually said about herself and her own dogmas rather than seeing them through an oftentimes erroneous and misunderstanding Protestant lens.

That made all the difference. And while I was in the process of deeply considering the Catholic Church, and taking some flak from Protestant friends for posting quotes from the Church Fathers, I declared the following publicly:

> To post quotes, questions, or points that affirm, in even the slightest way, Roman Catholicism is not to be a Roman Catholic. As of now, I am not.
>
> But what I have realized is what I have been, namely a deeply *prejudiced* man when it comes to the Catholic Church. There was so much theology and history I simply didn't know, and, to paraphrase Mark Twain, so much I knew that just wasn't so.
>
> If the process of shedding this prejudice leads me to Rome, so be it. I'm not afraid of where an earnest

search of truth, grounded in a love of Jesus, takes me. If it doesn't, I will no doubt be much the better for shedding my ignorance and prejudice in the process.

And by the time I was done shedding, I realized I was a Catholic.

Chapter Eight

Rushing to Meet Your Mother

Matthew Schmitz

Interviewed by Julia Yost

&

Julia Yost

Interviewed by Matthew Schmitz

Julia Yost is senior editor of *First Things*. She is a PhD candidate in English at Yale University and holds an MFA in fiction from Washington University in St. Louis.

Matthew Schmitz is senior editor of *First Things*. His writing has appeared in the *New York Times*, *Washington Post*, *Spectator*, and other publications. He holds an AB in English from Princeton University.

Julia Yost: *First, some background. What were your impressions of Catholicism while you were growing up evangelical in a small town in Nebraska?*

Matthew Schmitz: My grandparents on my father's side are Catholic, and I loved them, but I was concerned for their salvation. I had been raised to believe that Catholics were probably not Christians. Catholicism was a kind of thicket of superstition that one would get tangled in on the road to heaven. You had to clear it away by introducing people to their personal lord and savior Jesus Christ. So I tried to introduce my Catholic cousins to Christ. I even tried to witness to my grandparents. But I thought Catholicism was at odds with Christianity, and that impression was reinforced by the fact that the kids who went to the Catholic school were bullies.

What did they do? Did they throw rocks at you or something?

They called me "Jesus Boy," because I was so religious. I don't think they ever threw anything at me, though I punched one of them.

Say a bit more about the style of evangelicalism in which you were raised. You were baptized when and how?

When I was three years old, my mother was pregnant with my younger brother and I asked her if Jesus could come into my tummy just as my brother had come into hers. This was my inept way of saying I wanted to accept Jesus into my heart—an idea I would already have been introduced to. But it was also my first moment of Marian piety, however unwitting. Literally speaking, in that moment I took Mary as my model in faith. I asked to become a God-bearer like her, to become pregnant with Christ.

So your family was articulate about this moment of accepting Jesus into your heart, and pointed to that moment and said, "Matthew is saved"?

Yes, and I remained true to that decision. A decade later, at age thirteen, I was baptized in the Elkhorn River. It was a source of some anxiety of my grandparents that I wasn't baptized earlier.

Why were they concerned?

There's a lot of talk about how Catholics have something called the "sacramental imagination." Often this is said sentimentally, as if Catholics were romantic savages who view everything as suffused with wonderment and beauty, enchanted people who climb up and down the rungs of the analogy of being. This is a way of talking around the actual content of the Faith. What the sacramental imagination should mean, first of all, is actual belief in the sacraments: Marriage is indissoluble and ordained by God. Christ is present in the Eucharist and must be revered. My grandparents in their concern for my baptism were much better examples of the sacramental imagination than all the faith-in-fiction litterateurs combined. The sacrament of Baptism was real to them, and so long as I went without it, they feared my damnation. They had the sacramental imagination in that cold, narrow sense. My parents did not.

So you went to college then, at Princeton. And not long after you got to Princeton you ceased to be an evangelical. But before you went off to college, were there any rumblings of defection? Did you have a sense that there was something lacking, or something off, in the religion in which you had been raised?

At a young age, I went through something called the Gothard Seminar. Bill Gothard was a kind of evangelical moralist who would fill out stadiums in second- and third-tier American cities in the eighties. A lot of young, square

Americans would go to see him explain basic principles for how to live. You know, methods of conflict resolution, things like that, but it would all be "biblically derived." He had a very strong focus on following certain rules. And for the most part they were quite helpful. Most of the people who went to his seminars were fairly well grounded, not too prone to take too seriously what he was saying. You can listen to a man go on about this that and the other and take from this what you think is sound, and whatever you think is unhelpful you just set to the side.

But when I went through this, I was quite young, and I took it all very seriously. I came out of it as an incredibly legalistic and unhappy boy (though Gothard did help me overcome some of the vices of youth). I eventually rebelled against him and persuaded the elders of my church to stop patronizing his seminars. Like many people who say they are Christian, Gothard did not believe in grace. At this time I was seventeen. I was living in Washington, DC, working as a congressional page and attending Capitol Hill Baptist, pastored by Mark Dever. I met with Dever and spoke to him about my interest in Jonathan Edwards, on whom I was writing a paper. He gave me a book by J. I. Packer, and I became a Calvinist. I was young, restless, and Reformed.

At the same time, I began to read whatever struck me as both solidly "Christian" and undeniably great. So what are Christian things? Christian things would probably not be post-Reformation Catholic things, but they might be some older Catholic things. A lot of Protestants operate with a kind of unspoken idea of a subterranean apostolical succession, even a kind of ghostly Petrine office. Augustine is okay because he influenced Calvin, and after all, Luther was an Augustinian friar. So I read Augustine's *Confessions*, I purchased the *Institutes*, and though I read *Confessions*, I did not read the *Institutes*. I recently looked back at my copy of the *Institutes* and found my bookmark on page seventy, where I left off. That's as far as my Calvinism went. So all the Calvinists can mock me for being non-committal, and I accept the charge.

When I returned to Nebraska for my senior year, I was left with two intellectual problems. One was the reliability of Scripture, the other was evolution. I read the first three volumes of N. T. Wright's *Christian Origins and the Question of God* series. He writes big books, and they really were magnificent. They convinced me that Scripture is reliable and that historical criticism can be done in ways consonant with orthodox faith. That was the basic demonstration. I didn't have to enter into the minor arguments or pedantries and take sides and say, "I'm an N. T. Wright guy," or this, that, or the other. I just saw that someone working in a very scientific way could fully affirm the Christian inheritance.

What I couldn't really resolve was this evolution issue. When I arrived on campus at Princeton, I was still a young earth creationist. I believed that if one ceased to be a young earth creationist, one would cease to be a Christian. It had always been presented to me that way: Believe this or cease to believe at all. Slowly I began to let go of that. I had read Augustine and seen that he had a different way of approaching it. I was ready to follow.

What I didn't realize at the time was that I was ceasing to be a Protestant, at least to be a pure kind of Protestant. I was becoming a more complicated kind of Protestant, or a more Catholic kind of Christian. I was looking for ways of reading Scripture, which, though I wouldn't have put it this way at the time, were more traditional or ecclesial. But a strictly intellectual account is misleading. I was not locked in a cell wrestling with God all this time. I was pulling all-nighters, drinking beer, participating in the corruption on campus. The unhappiness that I found in that prompted me to keep thinking about my faith.

So you were evangelical still for a bit at Princeton?

One of the things going on when I was an undergrad was the instantaneous emergence of gay rights as the most important issue, bar none. That simply hadn't been the case when I was in high school. When I was in college, it was absolutely definitive. So if you supported gay rights, you became a liberal Protestant. If you were quiet about it or kind of tacitly supported it, you could remain an evangelical. After deciding that I couldn't accept gay marriage, I was confronted with the fact that my ideas of sex were incoherent. My friends asked me, "If I love someone, why can't I be with that person?" So I had to give a response. Well, St. Paul has some scathing things to say about that. He does, but did he have deep reasons for saying what he did? I read Elizabeth Anscombe's essay "Contraception and Chastity," in which she compares contraceptive sex to sodomy, and thereby articulates a view that is logically coherent and that also appealed to me sympathetically because it bound people of every proclivity. That appealed to my sense of fairness. It struck me very vividly that the Catholic Church had been right about this. How could they be right about it if they were wrong about everything? If it was the kind of beast or monster I had been raised to believe it was, how could it happen to be right about this? So I began looking into the Catholic Church.

How important was the Princeton Catholic milieu in making your conversion possible?

I ran into an acquaintance of mine from the evangelical fellowship late one night in the taproom of my eating club. He asked me how my walk with the Lord was going, and I said not very well. I had a conviction that I should become Catholic but was hesitating because it would demand things of me that I didn't want to give. He said that he was in the same position. And then I told him that we were both going to hell because we had been given a gift of understanding that we refused. So we resolved at that moment, in the midst of this terrible crowd, to enroll in RCIA. The next day we did.

Was that the end of it?

As soon as my reason was well disposed toward the Church, I could accept all the arguments and my objections dropped away. But my instinctual aversions remained. They had to be overcome more slowly. My most intense aversion was to Mary, who I'm sure was praying most intently, guiding me, even as I recoiled from her. So I would say that I didn't have an intellectual conversion, even though there were very serious intellectual issues behind it. I didn't really read my way into the Church. In the end, I just had to show up once a week, and be submissive and docile.

It's long been my sense that people don't really read or reason their way into or out of the Church, though they often claim to. The decisive factors are less rational, more experiential. For me, this is one of John Henry Newman's great themes. His Apologia pro Vita Sua *took the form of autobiography because he could not explain his religious opinions without telling his whole life story. Earlier, he had written a book, the* Essay on Development, *partly to see whether he could reason his way out of the Anglican Church and into the Catholic Church. The intellectual work he does here is very important, in making his conversion possible. But at the end of that book, he leaves his argument not quite complete, then tacks on a conclusion that says, "Time is short, eternity is long." This is his way of saying that at a certain point, you stop reasoning and take action. Even the most intellectual conversion is not reducible to reasons but is a matter of will, emotions, imagination—the things that compel action. As Newman wrote elsewhere, "Life is not long enough for a religion of inferences. . . . Life is for action."*

Tim Crane, an atheist philosopher, has a book called *The Meaning of Belief.* The book is based on the Bentham Lecture he gave to the British humanists a number of years ago. In this lecture, he challenges his fellow atheists, who he thought had been led off a philosophical cliff by Dawkins, Hitchens, and Dennett. The problem he saw in the New Atheists' arguments was that they assumed religion was simply a matter of cosmology, a certain conception of the way this whirligig is put together, or else a mere set of moral beliefs. Crane's point, which I think will seem obvious to any believer but clearly is not obvious to the people who are arguing furiously against religion, is that religion is something more. It involves cosmology and morality, yes, but it is more comprehensive and more practical. It is about a shared experience of God that allows one to identify with others through everyday practice. Ultimately I became Catholic just by beginning to view things in the way Catholics viewed them. All I had to do was relinquish my opposition.

What would you say to prospective converts today who are considering the Catholic Church for the reasons you did? This seems not the most auspicious hour for Catholics of your persuasion.

If you were a child who had been separated from his mother at a young age, and hadn't seen her for many years, and finally found where she was—but then learned she had a serious ailment—would you not go meet her for that reason? Say, "Well, it's not an auspicious time"? Of course you would rush to meet your mother.

But if your mother were about to get a sex change, to deny that she is your mother, and so become unrecognizable . . . ?

My faith is not shaken by what the pope is doing, though I have a very negative view of it. Many would say the pope isn't compromising the Church's teaching on marriage. I don't think that. I think the pope's doing it, and that if he fully and finally succeeded, the Church would be shattered. The Catholic faith would be falsified.

But we can look at history and see that there have been other moments when the main body of bishops has not defended Catholic doctrine or has even inclined toward heresy. That even the bishop of Rome has done this. So if one were prepared to become Catholic before but not after the regrettable events of 2016, one should have given up on the Church much earlier.

What is infallibility? Ultramontanes and anti-Catholics exaggerate the Church's claims to infallibility. Those claims are in fact very narrow: The Church will never require Catholics to believe that which is false. If you look back at the promulgation of the doctrine of the Immaculate Conception, it's very clear that Catholics are required to believe it. If you don't believe it, you are said to separate yourself from Peter, from Paul, from the saints, the martyrs, from all the apostles, down through the centuries. You have to believe in the Immaculate Conception to be Catholic. No such demand is being made with this pastoral approach to marriage. In fact, all of the language used to advance it deliberately avoids that kind of definition. If a real dogmatic redefinition were to happen, it would shatter the Church's claim to be what she is. It would show that she never existed.

Matthew: *But enough about me. You, too, had a sort of conversion during your college years.*

Julia: I underwent a sort of intra-ecclesial conversion, to traditional and dogmatic Catholicism. I was raised in the Church, but in a very suburban sector of it, very bourgeois. The parish mission song beseeched God to "Guide and unite us in our efforts / As we build community"—that should give you a sense of the tone. The architecture and liturgical aesthetics were as Protestant as possible, to a degree that I suspect was illicit. Heresy was not preached openly, but concerns were mooted about gender equality in the Church, and in fact the Creed had been emended in this direction. For instance, Christ had not "become man," but rather had "shared human life with us."

I went through this parish's CCD program, up through confirmation, which for us happened in eleventh grade. We learned in CCD that God is love, and I gleaned an impression that sexual morality is negotiable, though teen pregnancy is very bad. No one ever explained to me the importance of the sacrament of confession, or its relation to Communion. Basics of the sacraments were simply not part of the curriculum.

I remember one Sunday after my confirmation, attending a neighboring parish, where I occupied myself by reading the front matter in their missal. We didn't have missals in the pews at my home parish. In fact, we didn't have pews. And in this missal I came across the notion that Catholics "with knowledge of grave sin" must not receive Communion until they have confessed. I naturally thought the category of "grave sin" included murder, child abuse, and racism—probably nothing else. I thought that "knowledge of" meant "I know that my neighbor is beating his children." It would not be knowledge of one's own grave sins, because only well-behaved bourgeois people go to church.

So how did you end up where you are now?

I finally got catechized while in college. I was reading James Joyce, and I found in *Portrait of the Artist* and *Ulysses* a version of Catholicism that was totally alien to me—one that assumed that Catholics in the pews are grave sinners whose souls are in danger. The category of grave sin turned out to be much more capacious than I had thought. In short, it was time to stop profaning the Eucharist.

So it was in the library stacks that I learned how to profess the Faith in which I had already been baptized and confirmed. In a sense, I guess I did read my way into the Church. But I didn't reason my way. I was drawn in large measure by envy of Joyce, who had been raised in a Catholic Church that had spiritual and imaginative power, and that went on haunting him after he had left. I couldn't imagine writing an autobiographical novel to compare with Joyce's *Portrait*, about a young woman who grew up singing "On Eagle's Wings."

Well, if not a portrait, that's a striking snapshot of the artist as a young woman.

Chapter Nine

A Passion for the Truth: An Astronomer Discovers Chesterton

Karin Öberg

Interviewed by Nathaniel Peters

Karin Öberg is a Professor of Astronomy at Harvard University and leader of the Öberg Astrochemistry Group at the Harvard-Smithsonian Center for Astrophysics. Raised in Sweden, she received a Bachelor of Science degree at the California Institute of Technology and a PhD at Leiden University. She received a Hubble Postdoctoral Fellowship from NASA, is widely published, and serves on the board of the Society of Catholic Scientists.

Nathaniel Peters is the Executive Director of the Morningside Institute and a lecturer at Columbia University. He received a BA from Swarthmore College, an MTS from the University of Notre Dame, and a PhD from Boston College in the history of Christian thought and ethics. He has published articles and reviews in a variety of scholarly and popular venues.

Nathaniel Peters: *Tell us about your family. What were some of the traits that best characterized the Öberg household? Was your family religious at all?*

Karin Öberg: I grew up in Sweden and my family still resides there. Like many Swedish families, my family was not very religious, but held on to many religious customs and morals. As a baby I was baptized in the Swedish Lutheran Church, the state church at the time, and later I went to weekly Christian pre-school. My only memory of the latter is the time when I rejected the image of God as male and consequently drew him as a woman. My father, a self-proclaimed atheist and stoic, was quite proud at this early sign of freethinking and questioning of religious authority. My mother identifies as a Christian but does not go to church. Apart from brief evening prayers with her as a young child, I had little religious formation.

While not very religious, my family was and is vocally moral. It was clear from an early age that there are right and wrong actions and pursuits. We were given a strong intuition about the realism of morality, though little discussion of its origin. Pursuing truth and keeping promises were especially valued and that has formed me.

My parents also instilled us with a sense that you have a duty to do something greater with your life than serving yourself. There was an expectation to strive for excellence and to eventually pursue a career that gave something valuable back to the world. This also came through in books we read and the movies we watched. The first real book that I read was *The Lord of the Rings*. It was my first literary love and it remains one of the most formative books of my life. It gave me a taste for adventure and taught me the romance of self-sacrifice and duty. In a similar vein, we watched romantic—in the nineteenth-century sense of the term—movies where self-sacrifice for the greater good was an important part of the story, such as *A Tale of Two Cities* and many classic American and British WWII movies.

One of the things I've been struck by in our friendship is the good marriage your parents have. What effect do you think that had on you?

It is difficult to appreciate the gift of a stable and loving home if that is all you have seen, and I still think I am not grateful enough! My parents take the family seriously. Their respective careers were always family projects. My father started a company when I was seven, and my mother treated it like it was her responsibility too. When she wanted to leave teaching elementary school a few years later, my father made it clear that it was his concern as much as hers. They always faced problems together. That unity carried over into the rest of our family life. We always had dinner together, and we had real discussions at dinner. We kept three different encyclopedias on hand and used them frequently to prove each other wrong; we children took great pride the times we managed to claim victory against our father. There were also bitter losses, however, such as the time when one of my brothers was convinced that there were four archangels, but Encyclopedia Britannica claimed three, and Britannica always trumped.

What about the rest of your childhood? Did you find the intellectual and spiritual climate of Sweden to be nurturing or critical of faith?

Although I had no strong religious formation from my family, I took it for granted that God existed. When I was ten, someone in my class asked if I believed in God. I said, "of course," and I suddenly realized the answer wasn't "of course" for everyone. This was unsettling. Still I assumed that I believed in God for the next few years, until it came time to be confirmed in the Swedish church. About half the students in my class were confirmed, but most treated confirmation as a cultural rather than a religious event. I took it more seriously. I began my confirmation preparation in good faith believing in God. As the program proceeded, I came to realize that while I still found some form of philosopher's God reasonable, I could not take the God of the Bible seriously. This was almost an inevitable outcome of the program, I think, which focused on general spirituality and morals rather than on a serious understanding of the Bible. I asked my Lutheran confirmation pastor whether I should be confirmed if I sort of believed in God and didn't believe in Jesus. She said it was okay, and I got confirmed. In my heart I knew it was wrong, though, and I still feel bad about it to this day. By the time I turned fourteen or fifteen, I was an agnostic.

I think perhaps the most damning I can say about the religious climate in Sweden is that it was neither critical nor nurturing of faith. Sweden is very secular; during my childhood the only Christians I knew were a few Pentecostals and older Lutherans. However, this secularization manifested itself more as disinterest in religion than hostility toward it. Lutheranism was part of the cultural heritage; something harmless that was more of interest to older people. Otherwise there was little talk or thought about faith.

It seems like your family had strong intellectual interests as well as moral convictions. Did these help form you for your current vocation?

Yes. I got my first science books when I was learning to read, around age five or six. I got my first chemistry set a few years later—but alas my parents then realized I was too young and did not allow me to play with it! My father has degrees in chemistry and environmental science, and science discussions and problem solving was commonplace in the family; as part of our story time before bed, he held math competitions between my brothers and me.

What made you first interested in astronomy and chemistry?

As a child, I had broad interests and was generally good at school. I liked math from early on, but, thanks to my father's introduction of some well-chosen biographies of brilliant mathematicians, I realized early on that I was not a brilliant mathematician in the making. Instead I thought I might make a career out of combining science with my passion for the beautiful; that is, with art. Once I got to high school, some things crystallized. I was interested in many subjects: art, architecture, design, applied physics, but I had a natural intuition for solving chemistry problems. This was actually somewhat frustrating, as my main interest became physics and astronomy; I had by then become convinced that they presented the biggest questions and most interesting problems; that is, the greatest adventure. Being a realist, I still applied to college with the intent of doing chemistry; in high school I began to think about going to the US for college and ended up going to Caltech, hoping to find a way to apply chemistry to something that interested me. And I did in astrochemistry!

What were the religious or philosophical beliefs you had going through high school and college?

I didn't think much about religion in high school, at least not directly. I did sometime ponder my convictions that there is an absolute moral law, and that I do have a will that is in some sense free. Both of these truths are difficult to reconcile with a wholly materialistic worldview. I certainly did not manage to reconcile them. This discrepancy bothered me and continued to bother me as I started college.

A second step on my journey toward Christianity took place in College; at Caltech I got to know Christians my age who were thoughtful, intelligent people. That put the question of God back into my head. For no reason I can recall—and certainly not because I believed in Christ—by junior or senior year I began considering myself a Christian. I began wearing my confirmation cross again, which I hadn't done since my confirmation. In retrospect, I think this was less a sign of new faith than it was a challenge to God and to my peers to prove me right or wrong. One of the outcomes of wearing the cross was that some people assumed I had serious Christian convictions, an easy mistake! One such person started dating me and as a graduation gift he gave me C. S. Lewis's *The Screwtape Letters*. As he predicted, I liked it. Later that year, I started graduate school in astronomy in Leiden in the Netherlands. There I read Lewis's *The Abolition of Man*, which crystallized the struggles I had been having about moral absolutes and free will. More importantly, it began to propose a solution.

I'm still not sure what made me buy *Mere Christianity* by C. S. Lewis, but I read it in one sitting later that fall. Halfway through, I realized I believed what Lewis was saying, and I kept reading, trying to internalize the joy and the obligations that came with the belief. The solutions to my intellectual struggles were coming, but it was disorienting to be converted in an hour! I vividly remember spending most of the day reading a few paragraphs and then not being able to sit still, but getting up pacing about. And then not being able to stay away from the book for long and returning to the armchair to continue to read. By the end, I realized I believed in more than the philosophers' god from *The Abolition of Man*, I believed in the Christian God of *Mere Christianity*. Being a rational person, I googled for local, English-speaking churches—I am embarrassed to say I never learnt Dutch despite spending four years in the Netherlands—and I found the Anglican church in The Hague. Beyond its intrinsic qualities, it was appealing that I would be going to the Church of C. S. Lewis.

What was your life like as an Anglican?

For the next three years I was a Sunday church-goer at the Anglican church. I did not pray very much outside of church—occasional prayers of gratitude, perhaps, but no regimen of prayer on my own. Instead of praying, I read. My devotional life largely consisted of literature by authors with a strong spiritual leaning, including all the C. S. Lewis I could find. The first year was joyful and peaceful as I read myself deeper into the Faith. A year later I felt even quite comfortable in my newfound faith. Then one of my brothers gave me G. K. Chesterton's *Orthodoxy;* he told me that if I was going to be a Christian, I might as well do it right! I finished *Orthodoxy* in a second unsettling day. It was not a momentous conversion as the day of *Mere Christianity*, but rather a feeling of being understood and wanting more than my existing devotional life was providing.

Orthodoxy made me read more Chesterton, including his books on St. Thomas and St. Francis, and *The Everlasting Man*. While I remain incredibly fond of Lewis to this day, Chesterton speaks more directly to my heart. I think I experience the world very similarly, and it is a wonderful thing to read books by someone who sees the world the same way but can express it much more cleverly. This close affinity with Chesterton got me wondering whether I was in the right Church. My mind and heart had been well-formed for the Catholic way since childhood; up until my twenties I re-read Tolkien almost every year, and that year I began feeling drawn toward it with increasing strength.

By the time I returned to the US for a postdoc at the Harvard-Smithsonian Center for Astrophysics, where I now work, I was thinking about Catholicism more seriously. I didn't know any practicing Catholics, but I started playing with the idea of converting, mentioning it to some friends, testing the ground. For some time everything Catholic appealed to me: books, movies, symbols, and it became more and more difficult to push the idea of joining the Church out of my mind.

Tell us about why you decided to enter into full communion with the Catholic Church.

For me, the decision to become a Christian took an hour; the decision to become a Catholic took four years of grinding down resistance. Going to the Episcopal Church near Harvard pushed me over the edge. In Holland, I had a brilliant, passionate Anglican priest, who reminded me of C. S. Lewis. He was prolife, which upset many, and I suspected he had been exiled from a diocese in England because of this. With him as my shepherd, I felt no urgency to convert. That changed when I returned to America. People at the Episcopal Church I attended were very nice, but it became clear that it was not my spiritual home. There was a dissonance between the Nicene Creed they recited and what was actually believed that I could not comprehend. My passion is for the truth, and any place that lacks truth, that takes it lightly, or professes something with a wink is not for me.

One day in 2010 I made an appointment with a Catholic

priest and asked him how one converts, what the process is, how to discern whether it's the right thing to do. I had already gone to Mass at St. Paul's, the local Catholic Church, a few times to see what it was like. After a second appointment with another priest, I began RCIA. The priest leading the RCIA was the first practicing Catholic I knew. Then something miraculous happened. Part way into my RCIA program, a non-practicing dear friend begun her journey back to the Faith, and in a way we converted together. After completing St. Paul's two-year RCIA program, I was received into the Church the Easter of 2012.

Shortly thereafter I moved to UVA to take up a chemistry faculty position, and there I got to know and fell in love with the Dominican order. I suspect I was lead there by my confirmation saint, Catherine of Siena. Under the tutelage of the friars, I came to appreciate the Church's rich intellectual tradition, and their young adults group provided my first Catholic community. I only spend ten months in Charlottesville, but it was ten formative months.

What has your family made of your religious journey?

They were not thrilled when I announced my decision to convert. Modern Sweden rose out of the Reformation, and was confirmed by the thirty-year war, when Sweden lead the Protestant side. Many prejudices against Catholicism were formed over the centuries and many remain. For my family, especially for my grandparents, my conversion was a cultural betrayal. I had already abandoned my homeland, and now also the Protestant heritage. I was also not very good at explaining why I was doing it. I had good reasons to be a Christian, but at the time of my RCIA I did not have very good reasons to become Catholic. In the Catholic Church I simply felt at home and I knew in my heart that it was the right thing to do long before my mind understood why.

Five years later my family still do not completely understand why, but their love and loyalty to me has never wavered. Their loyalty to me now also to some extent includes the Catholic Church—none of my family members are pleased if you speak ill of the Church in their presence. My family was also instrumental for making my very Catholic wedding in Sicily a wonderful, wonderful day.

What has been most joyful and enriching about being a Catholic? Most challenging?

Very quickly after I converted it became difficult to remember I had not been Catholic since birth! The Church felt like home from the first time I went to Mass and being part of it felt natural. I take great joy in weekly Mass and daily prayer; these obligations have made my life richer and paradoxically freer. There have not been many external challenges. My own culpability has been much clearer, post-conversion—but love of the truth gives me an odd delight in seeing my own flaws more clearly.

Actually, there was one challenge: dating. I went on many, many first dates between starting RCIA and two years ago, and very few second ones. I frequently wondered whether I was being too particular in desiring someone who took his faith as seriously as I, or whether God was maybe trying to tell me that the single life would serve him best. God resolved that question for me when I met my husband in December of 2015.

How did you meet your husband?

My husband is from Brescia, in northern Italy. There it's not St. Nicholas or the Christ child, but St. Lucy who brings presents to children on her feast day. A few years ago, Davide was walking home and he realized that it was the night before St. Lucy's feast day. He thought back to his childhood and casually prayed, "St. Lucy, for so many years you brought me such wonderful gifts. This year, what if you were to bring me the best gift of all: a wife?" The next day he saw me at Mass and decided to introduce himself afterward. While we were talking, you, Nathaniel, came up to me and, knowing that St. Lucy is important in Sweden as well, wished me a happy feast day. Davide realized that St. Lucy might be answering his prayers! We were married two years later in the Duomo in Siracusa, the city where St. Lucy was born and martyred, and where some of her relics are kept. Three months later, the sensation is similar to post-conversion: being married to Davide feels so natural it is difficult to remember it has been only three short months, but there is also every day the thrill of the adventure, the unpredictability and lack of complete control that giving your life to another person entails.

How are you able to live your faith among your colleagues and students? Do you ever experience skepticism or hostility because of your faith?

It has been joyful and unfolded very naturally. Harvard is a secular place and people expect there to be opposition, but I have been open about my faith with students, colleagues, and administrators alike with no repercussions. For most people, my religion is a personal choice and not threatening. Some people find it interesting, and even an asset to have someone that they can discuss religious topics with or send religious students to for advice. This openness to my faith goes back to my recruitment from UVA. During one of my visits to Harvard, I told the department chair, who is an atheist, that I was concerned about leaving behind the only Catholic community I had known. He promptly arranged for Catholics at Harvard to contact me and try to convince me it would be good to come to Cambridge also as a Catholic!

An early decision that I made after becoming faculty was to be visibly Catholic. My office contains pictures of St. Thomas Aquinas and Mary, as well as a crucifix. I often wear my crucifix to work, always when teaching, so students know that I exist and they can contact me if they want. They have and this has allowed me to interact with Catholic and other Christian students across Harvard. I am especially happy that one of them is my godson.

How do you understand the relationship between the natural sciences and the Catholic faith?

There is only one truth and I do not believe there can ever be a real conflict between the truth uncovered by science on one hand, and by theology and revelation on the other. I further believe that the two paths can be mutually illuminating and supportive. Many theological quests implicitly or explicitly make assumptions about the cosmos we inhabit and how it has unfolded. Such theological endeavors should be enriched by a clear and up-to-date understanding of the scientific explanations and theories. Physics and biology show us that we live in an unfolding creation, which makes us think about God and creation differently; more beautifully I think. The scientific project fundamentally relies on the reality and intelligibility of the material world, and belief in the Christian God provides a rational reason for such assumptions. An ongoing dialogue between the two should be mutually beneficial, and would probably also help in resolving confusions on what questions science and theology are equipped to answer. There is a modern intuition that science and religion are naturally in conflict, which seem wholly false to me, and anything that can be done to expose this myth would be a step toward the truth.

What would you say to Catholic students who are interested in the natural sciences but are afraid that they will face difficulties because of their faith?

Be courageous, pursue your vocation, and trust in God. There is no guarantee that there won't be difficulties, but that is the case whatever profession you chose, and if you put God first and find a strong Catholic community, you will have the strength to face them. I do want to add that it is often prudent to be careful about sharing your faith at work at vulnerable career stages, and I believe that can be done without compromising your faith; once you are at a more comfortable stage of your career: be more open about your faith for the sake of those more junior to you.

What would you say to students who reject the Catholic faith because of the claims of some in the scientific community?

I do not think good scientific arguments against the Catholic faith exist. The two main objections against believing in God remain the problem of evil, and that there are sufficient natural explanations for reality. This was true when St. Thomas wrote his *Summa* and is true now. I think the progress in science has done little to undermine the counter arguments of St. Thomas and the philosophers and theologians that came before him.

My advice to students would then be, study the claims critically and seek out the counter arguments. If you search for the truth with an open and honest heart, I believe you will find it even if it for a short time may make you question God and the Church. I have many friends who are now very devout who during some years stepped away from the Church for different reasons. What all unites them is a hunger for the true, the good, and/or the beautiful. So perhaps: keep that hunger alive and do not be afraid to examine both the scientists and the Church teachings critically using the full power of your reason. In the end it will be a leap of faith whom to trust when reason can take you no longer. When that time comes, I find God as revealed by Christ to be the only answer that finally makes sense.

Chapter Ten

"How I Became the Catholic I Was"

Hadley Arkes

Interviewed by Cason Cheely

Hadley Arkes joined the faculty of Amherst College in 1966, and has been the Edward Ney Professor of Jurisprudence since 1987, assuming *emeritus* status in 2016. His many books include *The Philosopher in the City*, *First Things*, *Beyond the Constitution*, *Natural Rights and the Right to Choose*, and *Constitutional Illusions and Anchoring Truths: The Touchstone of the Natural Law*. His articles have appeared in professional journals, and in the *Wall Street Journal*, *Weekly Standard*, and *National Review*. He has been a contributor to *First Things*, a journal that took its name from his book of that title.

He was the main architect of the bill that became known as the Born-Alive Infants' Protection Act. The account of his experience is contained as an epilogue to *Natural Rights & the Right to Choose*. Arkes first prepared his proposal as part of the debating kit assembled for the first George Bush in 1988. Later, he led the testimony on the bill before the Judiciary Committee of the US House, passing in both the House and Senate in 2002. The second President Bush signed the bill into law with Professor Arkes in attendance.

At Amherst, he founded the Committee for the American Founding, a group of alumni and students seeking to preserve the doctrines of "natural rights" taught by the American Founders and Lincoln, and also a new center for jurisprudence, in Washington, DC, the James Wilson Institute on Natural Rights and the American Founding.

Cason Cheely is an attorney at Stone Crosby, PC. She resides with her husband, Dan, and their six children in the Philadelphia area where she serves on the Pastoral Council of the Archdiocese of Philadelphia and is involved with the CanaVox movement and Regina Angelorum Academy, a Catholic classical school. She received her JD *cum laude* from Notre Dame Law School in 2006 and her AB in the Woodrow Wilson School of Public and International Affairs at Princeton University in 2003. She studied Natural Law and Natural Rights with Professor Hadley Arkes at Princeton University during his tenure as a visiting fellow in the 2002–2003 academic year, and Professor Arkes advised her senior thesis entitled "Unto the Least of These: A Policy Framework for Embryo Adoption in the United States." She authored the chapter "Embryo Adoption and the Law" in *The Ethics of Embryo Adoption and the Catholic Tradition* (Springer, 2007).

Cason Cheely: *You have described your own conversion to Catholicism on April 24, 2010 as becoming that Catholic that you already were. When and how did this begin unfolding?*

Hadley Arkes: You give me the occasion to think back, and my story may be a version of my dear friend Richard Neuhaus's line, "on how I became the Catholic I was." I must have been settled into this long before I came across the aisle or crossed the Tiber. I had been curious about Catholicism, reading about it for many years, but I held back with the pull of my loyalties to my family, anchored in the Jewish tradition. My most serious inhibition came from a Jewish background, not from any incongruity in teaching, but out of a sense that I would be leaving the Jewish people. My wife's parents fled Vienna under Eichmann; her father's mother died in a camp. We have all of this, and it was difficult to deal with the curious understanding that I was defecting from the Jewish people, for I didn't have any such sense that I was defecting, or leaving the Jewish people.

Now just how I was led to take the last step is a bit of a story, and I'll step back to try to tell it. I don't have here what I usually have—an argument that unfolds—but rather mainly strands, and I'll try to weave them into a story that imparts the sense of things.

I was a student of Leo Strauss at the University of Chicago. But my friends who were tutored in these things insisted that, as I wrote more and more in exploring the logic of natural law, I was not writing as a Straussian—that my writing was in a Catholic vein, in a way that was not discernible to me at the time.

But it probably all began with thinking anew, thinking for the first time about abortion, in my late twenties, at the edge of thirty, with my dear friend and colleague from Amherst, Dan Robinson. I began to engage the matter in the style of principled reasoning that was woven into my own teaching, most notably that fragment that Lincoln wrote, in which he offered a model of what we may understand as a "principled" argument. He posed the question of how one could justify the enslavement of a black man:

> You say A. is white, and B. is black. It is *color*, then: the lighter having the right to enslave the darker? Take care. By this rule, you are to be slave to the first man you meet, with a fairer skin than your own.
>
> You do not mean *color* exactly?—You mean the whites are *intellectually* the superiors of the black, and, therefore have the right to enslave them? Take care again. By this rule, you are to be slave to the first man you meet, with an intellect superior to your own.
>
> But, say you, it is a question of interest; and, if you can make it your *interest*, you have the right to enslave

another. Very well. And if he can make it his interest,
he has the right to enslave you.[2]

We considered the force of the principled argument:
what is the ground on which you're removing a whole
class of human beings from the circle of rights-bearing
beings, just by switching the name—from child or person
to "fetus." I cited Paul Ramsey in *The Morality of Abortion*
edited by John T. Noonan, Jr. (1970)—tracing the development of the child in the womb, week by week, all the way
back to the zygote, no larger than the period at the end of a
sentence. And everything we have now genetically we had
at that moment. We know enough now to say that if the
zygote that was you or I had been destroyed, we wouldn't
have been the next pregnancy. If we draw on the model of
Lincoln's fragment, we would ask: what is the ground on
which you would say that the child in the womb is anything other than a human being? It doesn't speak yet? Neither do deaf mutes. It doesn't have arms and legs yet? Other
people lose arms and legs in the course of their lives without losing anything necessary for their standing as human
beings to receive the protections of the law.

Dan Robinson pointed out that this was the way the
Church reasoned about these things—with a combination
of embryology (i.e., empirical evidence) woven in with
principled reasoning of the natural law. In other words,
you didn't have to be Catholic in order to understand the
teaching on abortion, and that was indeed the teaching of
the Church—that was not a matter of faith or belief, but
the moral reasoning accessible to ordinary folk.

All of this led to the recognition that was so decisive: that
the Church had become the main refuge for natural law

---

[2]   *The Collected Works of Abraham Lincoln*, ed. Roy P. Basler (New

reasoning, which is to say, moral reasoning, at a time when currents of relativism were corroding all institutions, even the churches. That the Church stands against the currents and the culture, *contra mundum*. And my betting was the Church had it right. The Church has seen it all. As Fr. Jim Burtchaell used to say, the Church lifts a mirror to put in one's face, saying "this is what you're going to look like a dozen years from now if you proceed on this path." There are no surprises. The Church was and is the main refuge for sanity.

When I was your student at Princeton, where you were a visiting professor from fall 2002 to spring 2003, I had just been received into the Catholic Church on Easter 2002. Your class was one of the most, if not the most, significant classes I took in solidifying my own conversion. And you weren't Catholic yet at that point.

For a long time before becoming Catholic, I found myself in the curious position of explaining the Catholic position on different issues to people I met who were Catholic but were apparently in a haze about the teachings of the Church. I was at the Newman Bookstore at Catholic University a few years ago when a fellow came into the store and said to the manager that one book you really should have here is *First Things* by Hadley Arkes. The curious thing is that people would read me and assume I was a Catholic. There was apparently something in my manner of writing that was recognized by people who grew up in the tradition, something they saw as Catholic. They had seen something that I hadn't quite seen.

In that vein, I did years ago for *Crisis Magazine* a piece

Brunswick: Rutgers University Press, 1953), vol. III, p. 222 (speech at Peoria, October 16, 1854).

called "Jackie Robinson and the Ordination of Women." It began with a trivia quiz of baseball movies: Ronald Reagan played the role of Grover Cleveland Alexander on the Cubs, Dan Dailey played the role of Dizzy Dean on the St. Louis Cardinals, Jimmy Stewart played Monty Stratton of the White Sox, and who was it who played Jackie Robinson in the Jackie Robinson Story in 1952? And the answer was Jackie himself; Jackie had to play himself. Why? Because there were no black leading men in Hollywood at that time. But Lena Horne was there; why didn't they do it in cross-gender? As the answer went, You've got to be *faithful to the Jackie Robinson story*, and Jackie was a male. Well, listen, if you think God was incarnate, became human, he couldn't be an hermaphrodite; he had to come back as one or the other, male or female. If the priest is supposed to stand in the person of Christ, then, as the Congregation for the Doctrine of the Faith explained, there has to be some natural sign or symbol—he has to be male. And all of this could be said without denigrating the place of women in the Church as theologians and teachers, and objects of reverence, most notably of course with Mary. I wrote all this well before I became a Catholic.

There's a line in the Talmud saying that for forty days the embryo is just water. David Novak says nobody takes that seriously with what we've learned from modern biology. But of all things, a notable professor of political philosophy raised that point from the Talmud years ago in a meeting in Princeton; he was trying to make the point that there are many things that divide us that can't be bridged through the use of reason: you regard the embryo as human life, and Jews don't, he said. Michael Pakaluk turned that around and said, "That thing about the embryo being mainly water, do you take that as *true*? Are you willing to face up to

the implications of that position? For if the embryo is just
water, water can't be killed." And that accomplished teacher
of political theory *just avoided answering.* Could he really
think the embryo is just water? That's a real difference with
the Catholics. Catholics are willing to face hard scientific
evidence also to ask if any argument brought forth seriously on this issue has the sovereign attribute of being *true.*
Many people, even educated people, don't seem able even
to reason about the issue of abortion any longer.

I spoke at a black-tie affair in North Carolina in 1996, at
the time of the presidential election. I could tell the nature
and leanings of the group and I said, "Look, I haven't said
anything about the issue of abortion or made the argument to you tonight. But might I ask you simply to engage
your imagination in this way: If 1.3 million members of a
minority group could be lynched in this country every year
without the restraint of the law, where would you rank that
on the list of the issues of the day? Would it be just below
the issues of interest rates and unemployment? Would you
be surprised if I told you that I couldn't regard that as
a secondary issue but as a preeminent or central issue?"
Someone who sees the world in this way could simply not
help regarding abortion as an issue of the first order. For
from the answer to that question, many other rights and
claims will spring. The problem made me think of George
W. Bush who came in for a meeting with Fr. Neuhaus as he
was preparing to run for president in 1999, and he report-
edly said, "I'm with you on abortion, I just can't take the
lead." How much he meant that was shown when he never
even endorsed our Born Alive Infants Protection Act. The
endorsement came from the executive office of the president. But as that line of his lingered—that he couldn't take
"the lead" on this matter—I had wondered: would he have

said the same thing if a million members of a minority group were being lynched each year? Would he not have been moved to say something, even taken the lead as president in setting the national tone. But then what was the difference? Did he not really think that those lives taken in abortion were real *human* lives?

So, in matters of this kind, I could say, "This makes perfect sense to me, and I'm not even Catholic." I would keep reinforcing the sense then that the Catholic teaching on the issues of "life" isn't an appeal solely to faith, but that it is a powerful exercise in reason, weaving together both evidence of science and the force of principled reasoning.

As a number of friends would say, "Here's my friend Hadley, he defends the position of the Church—and he's not even Catholic." And that was taken as another way of pointing out that the position of the Church is offered as a claim of reason, not an appeal to faith. My early experience of the Church was the experience of being incorporated into the pro-life movement starting in the late 1970s. I was being welcomed in Catholic circles—they made a fuss over me, saying, "See, you don't have to be Catholic to understand the position of the Church."

I had never taught explicitly about religion, but apparently the accent on moral truths, objective truths grounded in nature and accessible to our reason, had confirmed for my Catholic friends, in an appealing way, what the Church had been trying to teach. Here, as in many instances, we find people drawn to the compelling force of the teaching, and then led from there to the Church that has become the main refuge of reason and sanity in our own time.

One of the most touching parts of this experience has been the letters coming in from former students explaining how the work we had done in the classroom many years earlier had brought them back to the Church.

Were there any particularly compelling moments in the lead-up to your becoming a Catholic?

The beckoning of the Church has always come through the welcoming face of friends, who have represented to me the body of the Church. I felt at home in that community—the body of Christ—long before I actually became a Catholic. Sometime in the 1970s, it dawned on me that, as I looked about, the people around me who took my own interests as though they were their own, who worried about me, supported me, persistently read what I wrote, they were Catholics. And more and more, they represented to me what it meant, concretely, to lead a Catholic life.

Perhaps the earliest revelatory moment came at a meeting of the Catholic Scholars Association nearly twenty years ago. The speaker, in one session, was Stewart Swetland, who had converted when he had been a student at Oxford, and he said that the turnabout sprang from his conversations with Robby George and Dermot Quinn. I was sitting with Robby at the moment when Stewart said that, and Robby was surprised to hear his remark. As he recalled, Stewart had been resisting them steadily. When I caught up with Stewart and told him of Robby's reaction, he said that it was really Dermot who had said the words that finally sparked the move. According to Stewart, Dermot had said that you can believe everything the Church tells you and not be a good Catholic. The question was, "Do you believe in the Church as a truth-telling institution?" And I thought at once, "I do, I really do. As I've said, when the Church stands *contra mundum*, against the currents of moral opinion on any issue, my betting is that the Church has it right.

Years later, at a dinner in Boston, Cardinal Law heard I was there and asked someone to bring me up. He said, I don't know how you do this at Amherst, and then said, "You know when Richard Neuhaus came into the Church, we thought you were coming in too." And I said, "Yes, you see the problem is we thought Richard was arranging a *group rate*. We thought we were getting some kind of deal." I dodged the question, but Cardinal Law became a good friend, and he never relented in his interest in bringing me into the Church. I was deeply touched by his interest in bringing me over.

I actually came into the Church after Richard Neuhaus died—he died in 2009. I remember when he came into the Church; we were all there at Dunwoodie seminary in New York. Cardinal O'Connor said, "You don't deserve this Richard any more than I deserve to be ministering it to you." It was a touching moment.

So I was on the outskirts looking in. I was always asking questions and reading on matters of theology. I had fallen into the habit of going to Mass at the Catholic Information Center with friends—out of interest, to see what the teaching was about and how it was taken in daily in the rituals and lives of friends. One day Robert Royal came into the Catholic Information Center, and I found myself saying something like, "Bob, what are you doing here? This isn't your parish!" Bob would turn that into the loveliest joke in later years, for he found the question touching and funny at the same time. He responded, "I know what *I'm* doing here. But what are *you* doing here?" That encounter with Bob brought home to me just how absorbed I was in the question of the Church, for I was acting as though I was already in it. It occurred to me that I simply assumed that

I belonged there at that point. And it really never occurred to me that people would wonder why I was there

Then, in October 2009, after the Red Mass at St. Matthew's Cathedral, Judy and I were on our way over to lunch at the Hilton to catch up with the Scalias. And then we encountered, on the way, Fr. Arne Panula. I had met him in New York years ago at the Opus Dei House, and he had just come into town to take over the Catholic Information Center. He was a dynamic figure, he took that Center to a new vibrancy and visibility, especially for young Catholic professionals who had landed in Washington. But at this moment, in October 2009, quite unexpectedly, he confronted me: "You, the most notable figure still standing at the threshold, trying to come to a judgment on the Church—what has been holding you back?!" Challenged there on the spot, I dipped into my Bert Lahr repertoire from *The Wizard of Oz*: I said, "C-c-c-courage. It's what put the ape in apricot. It's what I haven't got." I was channeling Lahr as the Cowardly Lion. And I thought, *Phew! I got out of that one.* I deflected Fr. Arne that time. But I was back at the CIC a few weeks later. I had gone to Mass with my friend, Luis Tellez, in from Princeton. Fr. Arne wasn't expecting me, but he noticed me there, and he said in his homily that the one strand connecting the two readings that day was . . . "C-c-c-courage." I thought: a good line. But when I greeted him at the end of the Mass, he said, "You notice, I *was* quoting you." And of course he was right; it was time for me to stop stalling. "All right, I said, let's have lunch and map this out." The following spring, on April 24, 2010, a Saturday—the same month and day that St. Augustine came into the Church—I came into the Church in a lovely Mass at the Catholic Information Center with Fr. Arne presiding.

As Midge Decter said long ago, "There comes a time when you should really join the side you're on."

Robby George said, "Why don't you let your friends know that you're coming in to the Church. Your friends would want to know about it." I thought that this was a small affair that should not occasion much noting. But I was astonished by the friends who came in from distant places—and astonished by the way that the news spread on the net. My beloved Judy was very much affected as she saw our friends coming up for communion, with more than eighty friends who in that intimate chapel.

How have your Jewish family members received the news of your Catholicism?

In general, my family never has understood my position on abortion; they see it as some religious doctrine of Catholics. One dear cousin found out my becoming a Catholic through the news stories. She wrote me an earnest letter asking why I had left the religion of our family. And I wrote back to her, asking about an uncle who scoffs at religion and never goes near a synagogue: Have you ever asked him why he's abandoned the religion of our family? Why is it that a Jewish atheist continues to be Jewish and hasn't abandoned the religion of our family? If there can be a Jewish atheist, surely there can be a Jewish Catholic. And the curious thing is I haven't felt less Jewish since I've been in the Church. Fr. McCloskey said once that Catholicism is simply a way of rendering universal the teaching in the Hebrew Bible, Jewish teaching. Michael Novak used to say when you're Catholic you're at least Jewish. And John Paul II famously said Jews are our older brothers in the faith.

The New Testament is predicated of course on the Old Testament. I can recall our dear friend, the late Cardinal

Francis George, discussing five instances of God revealing himself, four of which occurred, as he pointed out, in the Old Testament: the covenant with Abraham, the deliverance of the Hebrews from Egypt, the laws given to Moses, the guidance and warnings to the prophets. And finally, the fifth instance is the advent and resurrection of Jesus. As the Creed says, "On the third day, he rose again in fulfillment of the Scriptures."

You have said that belief in the Church as a truth-telling institution is what brought you in.

I had come into this matter of my conversion through the Church. The ready invoking of Jesus, I must confess, has not come readily to my lips. But as my friend Robby George pointed out, my story here bears a resemblance to other converts like G. K. Chesterton, who were drawn to the Catholic faith through the Church. And, as Cardinal Francis George put it, belief in the Church is part of the conviction of Catholicism. Cardinal George recounted in his book an encounter with a nice, earnest evangelical lady he met on an airplane who asked him, "Well, do you believe in Jesus as your Savior?" He wrote:

> She could not grasp the width, the expansion, of the act of faith in the Catholic Church, which is so much more inclusive than simply a faith that Jesus is our personal savior. Our faith includes also our understanding of the Church herself as a part of divine revelation. Nor could she understand, as she saw it, the formalism of the Catholic way of being disciples, even though she recognized the good will of

the people to whom she had very generously come to share her faith. She was puzzled by it.[3]

He later reflected that, when she'd asked whether he had been saved, he should have said, "Yes, I've been saved by Christ, but within a sacramental system that demands my free participation."

The historicist mentality has taken strong hold among us, but at the same time, ordinary folk have an awareness in common sense of certain truths, grounded in nature, that will not alter with time. Even in this age of animal rights, we don't find ourselves making labor contracts with our horses and cows, or seeking the informed consent of our household pets before we authorize surgery upon them. But we continue to think that those beings who are capable of giving and understanding reasons deserve to be ruled with a rendering of reasons in a regime that elicits their consent.

Instead of getting drawn then into the fashions of the day, perhaps our political men and women might find a better grounding for themselves if they could make their way again to a certain surety about those primary things that will not alter with time. And they may find in that way, as G. K. Chesterton used to say, that the Church offers us this liberation: it frees us from the tyranny of being children of our own age.

Churchill remarked once that the technology and equipment around us will change, including the technology for warfare and for interplanetary travel; and yet the main questions will remain the same. They are questions about the ends or purposes of human life: Why are we here? What purpose is disclosed in the arc of our lives? Are

---

[3]   *The Difference God Makes*, p. 213.

our lives composed of disconnected emotional episodes? Or are there principles which connect our acts, even as various as they are, and impart a sense of moral coherence? Those questions, Churchill said, spring from those ancient cities of Jerusalem and Athens. And, as he wrote, "It is this fact [the endurance of those questions and the human condition] more wonderful than any that Science can reveal, which gives the best hope that all will be well." We would put it another way: we can have this assurance with a clearer mind that what the Church teaches now, against moral fashions of the time, it will continue to teach "as it was in the beginning, is now, and ever shall be, world without end. Amen!"

It is the hold on those permanent things that offers us the ground of hope that all things may yet be well. We are not guaranteed success, even if we deserve success, for example, in standing up trying to protect innocent life. But if someone asks us in later years what we spent our time doing, we can give an account. We don't have to suffer any misgivings about whether we had been committed all these years to the right things, to the permanent things, to the things then so eminently worth doing.

Chapter Eleven

Ecumenical Devotion: Coming Home by Standing Still

Timothy Fuller

Interviewed by Matthew J. Franck

Timothy Fuller, born in Chicago in 1940, is a professor of political theory at Colorado College, a liberal arts college in Colorado Springs, where he has taught since 1965. In a career of wide-ranging teaching and scholarship in political philosophy, Fuller has focused most of all on the work of English thinkers from Thomas Hobbes to Michael Oakeshott.

Matthew J. Franck is Associate Director of the James Madison Program and Lecturer in Politics at Princeton University, Senior Fellow at the Witherspoon Institute, where he directs the Simon Center on Religion and the Constitution, and Professor Emeritus of Political Science at Radford University, where he chaired the department and taught courses in political philosophy, constitutional law, and American politics. He has written, edited, or contributed to books published by the University Press of Kansas, Lexington Books, Oxford University Press, and Cambridge University Press, and has published articles and reviews in *American Political Thought*, the *Review of Politics*, the *Journal of Church and State*, the *Catholic Social Science Review*, *National Affairs*, *The New Atlantis*, *First Things*, the *Weekly Standard*, the *Claremont Review of Books*, *National Review*, and *Public Discourse*.

Fuller's focus on English thought seems to have come naturally to him. His parents, natives of Massachusetts who moved to Chicago's north shore suburb of Winnetka, came from a long line of Episcopalians in the decidedly Anglo-Catholic branch of that church, and were active at every level from the parish to the diocese to the national conventions of the Episcopal Church. Fuller himself, when he was a boy at St. Luke's Episcopal Church in Evanston, began to sing in the choir at the age of seven, and continued until he left for Kenyon College—itself an Episcopal institution where he regularly attended chapel and led a student group, the Kenyon Christian Fellowship. In graduate school at Johns Hopkins University in Baltimore, Fuller worshipped at Mount Calvary Episcopal Church, an Anglo-Catholic parish that has recently entered the Ordinariate of the Chair of St. Peter, thus becoming a parish of the Roman Catholic Church.

Fuller met his wife, Kalah, during his graduate studies at Johns Hopkins. She too was a cradle Episcopalian, and they were married in her Maryland parish fifty-four years ago. Together, they became Roman Catholics in 2007, being received into the Church at St. Mary's Cathedral in Colorado Springs.

No crisis or precipitating event propelled Fuller into the Roman Catholic Church. But in his own description, he was "from an early age a student of church history and theology." Beginning in his teenage years, he read seriously in both areas and was particularly "interested in the causes of the split in the Church." Brought up in the Anglo-Catholic Church, he had been taught that there were three branches of the church: the Roman Catholic, the Eastern Orthodox, and the Anglo-Catholic. "In my family, we never thought of ourselves as Protestant. I was brought up to think of myself as a Catholic Christian within the Episcopal Church. So Methodists and Presbyterians and so on were Protestants, but we were not. Now that's not a universal feature of the way Episcopalians think."

But Fuller also learned fairly early that the Roman Catholic Church "had essentially rejected any claims of the Episcopal Church to the Catholic tradition." So he became interested in learning "whether the Catholic critique of the Anglicans was valid. And I came to the conclusion at that time that the claims of the Anglican tradition *could* be defended against those critiques." But over the years, he also came to understand that "what I was defending was decreasingly what the Episcopal Church was willing to defend."

Eventually this would become an intolerable chasm for Fuller—between what he viewed as the authentic claim of Anglicanism to be part of the Catholic tradition and the deteriorating commitment of the Anglican communion in practice to staking that claim, let alone to making good on it. But this chasm would take many years to widen to the point where it became intolerable. Meanwhile Fuller cherished hopes for a genuine ecumenism—a restoration of the shattered unity of the Church.

One of the features of the Anglo-Catholic point of view is a desire for ultimate reunion of the divided Church. And things looked very promising at the time of the Second Vatican Council, when the then-Archbishop of Canterbury, Michael Ramsey, met with Paul VI, and the International Commission on Reunion was created. Things for the moment looked very promising, and then it became clear to me increasingly after that that the Episcopal Church was turning away from that direction, and so part of what led to [my conversion] was the belief that if you're strongly committed to ecumenical reunion, the greater desire for that reunion lay with the Eastern Orthodox and Roman Catholics. And . . . I considered the Eastern Orthodox alternative . . . and as attractive as it is in many ways, I decided that what I was really in tune with was the ancient tradition preserved in the Roman Catholic Church. That's part of what led to the decision. I wouldn't call it a crisis so much, as, over the years, an increasing awareness that the things I was committed to were more deeply considered in the Catholic tradition and decreasingly considered in the Episcopal Church.

Oddly enough, the Episcopal Church, or at least some branches of it, has come to appear more Catholic rather than less in some of its practices. Fuller observes that since the Oxford Movement of the nineteenth century, "the Episcopal Church has become in a liturgical sense much more Catholic than it was at one time. But it's a curious feature that as it has become more Catholic in its liturgical practices, such as, for example, making communion the principal service every Sunday, as opposed to the old idea that it was once a month and so on, in other respects it has departed further from the Catholic tradition."

Those departures were stark ones in terms of doctrine and moral theology. Referring to the Lambeth conference held by the Anglican bishops every ten years or so, Fuller remarks, "In 1930, you could say that in terms of essential doctrine and moral teaching, there was virtually no difference between what the Catholic Church was defending and what the Anglican communion was defending. But that was the year in which they began to move towards changing their views both on divorce and, ultimately, on abortion," in the latter case with the conference's first steps toward approval of artificial contraceptives.

These were prime examples of a growing problem and posed grave obstacles to any prospect of healing the historic rifts in the Church. "If you're committed to an ecumenical reunion in the faith . . . it was no one of those issues that precipitated the change, but in my case, if you cared about trying to repair the rifts that have existed since the Reformation, you needed to pay attention to what the two greatest branches of the tradition maintained—namely, the Eastern Orthodox and the Roman Catholic Church—and it seemed to me that *not* to take seriously what they had to say about these things represented a kind of indifference to the question of reunion. And I would put it that way, more than that any single issue was the driving force."

Despite these doctrinal changes in Anglicanism, the Roman Catholic Church continued—and in notable respects continues to this day—to show a special solicitude toward the Anglican Church. As Fuller puts it:

> In a way, the Anglo-Catholic development in the twentieth century was initially quite heartened by the Second Vatican Council, because at that council they made a distinction between the Anglican communion and other Protestant denominations, and said that it was a special case. And I think historically it's true that the Catholic Church has always had a particular concern for the Church of England because in some ways, I think they've always looked back upon it as one of the great failures to have preserved the

relationship with the Church in England. I think you
can see that in people like John Paul II and Benedict,
who made special efforts to reach out to disaffected
Anglicans—the creation of the Ordinariate and other
things of that sort—which show that they had particular hopes for that development, and of course that
hasn't worked out in the way that it was hoped at the
time of the Second Vatican Council.

Through the creation of the Ordinariate of the Chair of
St. Peter (and similar national ordinariates in the UK and
elsewhere), the Vatican has been able to accommodate not
only individual conversions to Rome but whole parishes
and communities of Anglicans that have come in as a body.

Tim and Kalah Fuller were received into the Catholic
Church five years before the Ordinariate was created in
the United States. They had experienced a "peculiar division between the desire for reunion on the one hand, and
the increasing separation on certain traditional views on
which there had essentially been unanimity up until that
time." The defense of the Christian tradition, they came
to believe, "was more likely to maintain itself" in Roman
Catholicism than in Anglicanism.

But Fuller adds something else. "One thing that became
increasingly important to me too was what I'll call the
defense of the western tradition, by which I mean more
than just theological issues. I mean the defense of the central features of western civilization. And as that has become
more problematic in our time, I was saying to myself, where
is there a stout defense of the great traditions that go back
to classical and early Christian times, and the great defender
of that tradition is of course the Catholic Church."

It grieved him to see the direction being taken in the

church of his fathers. "One of the things that did bother me was that the Episcopal Church became an *advocate* of things like abortion," having begun by merely tolerating it, and "there were bishops in the church saying things like it was wrong to have children . . . buying into the radical ecological point of view, climate change and those things, that reducing population was a goal." Other bishops said things like "if we don't like something in the scriptures, we just change it."

Fuller relates the story of a friend who converted to Anglicanism who went to see his priest to discuss some difficulties he was having with accepting parts of the Nicene Creed, and (according to his friend) the priest said, "Well that's okay, most of it is poetry, and you can either say it with that in mind, or you can just not recite those parts of the Creed that you have trouble with." Fuller asked his friend, "Do you think that's a good way to look at what you're doing? What does it mean to be converted to the Episcopal Church under those circumstances? He had no particular answer to that other than that he wanted to belong there." Things like this were "indicative of the problem there more than any single issue" such as divorce or abortion.

While the drift of the Episcopal Church, and of the worldwide Anglican communion of which it is a part, continued apace, Fuller was reading his way to Rome.

> [John Henry] Newman was a very important figure. I had studied the Oxford Movement for a long time, and I was very familiar with his writings as well as Pusey and Keble and other figures who were central to the Catholic revival in the Anglican communion in the nineteenth century. Newman was extremely important, because when I read, for example, the

Apologia [*Pro Vita Sua*], where he describes a lot of what led to his conversion, I was thinking to myself, well you know, he's really describing *me* in many ways. Our circumstances were quite different in certain important ways, but the way in which he was reasoning about what led him to change struck me as having a very strong analogy to my own way of thinking.

Was he interested in the thought of any of the prominent later converts, such as Robert Hugh Benson, G. K. Chesterton, and Ronald Knox? "Of those three," Fuller says, "maybe Knox. The whole family was a whole set of distinguished people who came out of the Anglican tradition. And while I've always admired Chesterton as a writer, unlike a lot of people I don't make a big cult out of Chesterton. Benson strikes me as a very eccentric character." He would not call any of them particularly influential. "Newman stands out."

Fuller adds, "I was also interested in some of the later Anglican theologians who didn't convert but expressed a very Catholic point of view. Someone like Michael Ramsey, who was one of the great archbishops of Canterbury of the twentieth century, and who was very devoted to the ecumenical movement, and who I think was very disappointed after Vatican II that the chances for that reunion were going to diminish rather than increase."

He also cites the English Benedictine monk Gregory Dix, "the great Anglican theologian and student of liturgy," and author of *The Shape of the Liturgy*. "He also wrote a very stout defense of the validity of Anglican orders, back in the 1940s, which I found extremely convincing."

As an Anglo-Catholic, Fuller had always been deeply

interested in "whether the Anglican Church had maintained the apostolic succession." He explains:

> In terms of a purely historical fact, there's no doubt
> that the Anglican communion preserved the apostolic succession in the sense that you can trace an
> unbroken line from current bishops back to the apostolic world. The real issue between the Anglicans and
> the Roman Catholics wasn't about the historical fact
> of succession but whether at the time of the Reformation in England the Anglicans had substantially
> redefined the *meaning* of the apostolic succession, that
> they had departed from the traditional sacramental
> understanding of orders. That's a controversy which
> remains right down to the present time. And it was
> precipitated partly because in 1896 Pope Leo XIII
> issued an encyclical in which he declared Anglican
> orders null and void. Not that that was a departure
> from what the Catholic Church had maintained
> before that, but it was a pretty blunt rejection of
> what was at the time the beginning of this desire for
> reunion in the Anglo-Catholic world. And to that the
> then-archbishops of York and Canterbury wrote an
> episcopal letter in refutation of that encyclical.

One of the results of this, says Fuller, had been the
attempt at Vatican II and in the years since to "get beyond
that kind of 'you're no good' versus 'yes, we are good' argument." But the seeds sown at the Second Vatican Council
have not borne fruit.

As his reading and study took him further into the competing claims of Rome and Canterbury, Fuller also came to be highly influenced by the pontificate, and the writings, of Pope St. John Paul II. As a faculty member at Colorado College, he directed some students' theses on Catholic social teaching.

> And that led me back to Leo XIII, who in many ways inaugurates the groundwork for modern Catholic social teaching. I had studied his encyclicals pretty substantially, and then sort of traced a number of the issues addressed in that development over the next hundred years, leading down to *Centesimus Annus*, John Paul's review of Catholic social teaching on the hundredth anniversary of *Rerum Novarum*. But I also have read more widely in terms of things like *Fides et Ratio* and pretty much the whole range of what John Paul wrote. I don't have any question that he is—it seems to me easy to say that he is—the greatest modern papal theologian. I don't see anyone else who comes even close to him. *Veritatis Splendor* . . . I mean I could mention all sorts of examples of it. And he was extremely influential, because from my point of view, in reading his work, I could see that he understood political and economic issues with considerable profundity, and his ability to express the traditions of Catholic teaching in a way that was both completely in line with the tradition and also informed by all the modern developments in political and moral philosophy . . . I mean, it was really quite extraordinary.

After leaving an Episcopal Church riven by controversy and conflict, Fuller did not of course find himself in a Catholic Church where harmony and consensus reigned. But he never expected that. "Because of my long study of the history of the Church in general, I had no illusions about what the Catholic Church was going to be like. I didn't for a moment ever entertain the idea that somehow a different kind of human being was in the Catholic Church than in any other church."

Today in the Catholic Church, many of the controversies among the faithful break out over the words and deeds of Pope Francis. Fuller has kept up with Francis's writings, "and what I'd say is that I find him a very ambiguous writer. I find it a lot of times very difficult to know what it is that he's maintaining. That of course encourages people to take sides and to assume that they have an expert understanding of what he's trying to argue. In some ways I think he's contributed to this kind of controversy in part because if you read his writings carefully it's not always clear where he's wanting to go."

But this is no great cause of concern for Fuller. "I didn't come into the Catholic Church in order to live in a world where all was at peace and nobody ever disagreed with each other, because I don't think that's possible for human beings."

The manner in which Tim and Kalah Fuller finally came into the Church is quite a story all by itself. As he tells it:

> My wife and I agreed that this is probably what we should do. So we made contact with St. Mary's Cathedral here in Colorado Springs, which is actually in our neighborhood and therefore is our parish. We contacted the woman who runs the RCIA there, and the parochial vicar, who is a wonderful old Jesuit priest, and we met the two of them for a conversation. And we went through the usual things: we

showed them our baptismal certificates, and the first question they asked us was, were we both in agreement on this, because I'm sure there are lots of cases where one member of a couple wants to do it and the other one isn't so sure. We said no, no, we're at one. Then they said, do you have any reservations about the Catholic Church? And we said no. So they tried to figure out if we knew anything, and I said, well, I had read the entirety of the Catechism of the Catholic Church. The two of them said wow, we haven't done that! So then the next question was, do you have any problems with what you read there? And I said, no, no, we're okay on that. Our attitude was that we shouldn't do this until we were pretty ready to say no, we weren't going to put any conditions on this.

Fr. Bob, the Jesuit parochial vicar, began to change the subject, and he asked me if I knew anything about Gerard Manley Hopkins, which I realized immediately was an interesting question because Hopkins was an Anglican who had converted to the Catholic Church, and then become a Jesuit priest, and then of course a famous poet. So I said yeah, I'm an enthusiast for Hopkins, and for about a half an hour we talked about Hopkins' poetry more than anything else.

So at the end of all this, they said you two seem to be catechized already, so you don't have to go through RCIA. They said, all you have to do is go to confession, and if you do that this week, then we can receive you into the Church next Sunday morning. And that's what happened. We went to confession, and the next Sunday we stood up in front of the congregation at St. Mary's Cathedral and were received into the Church. . . . It's a true story!

Perhaps the most interesting thing about Tim Fuller's conversion is that he hardly moved at all. That is, he seems to have stood still, studying the faith of his fathers, scrutinizing the evolutions of the Catholic-Anglican relationship, and deepening his Christian commitment year by year, while the Anglican world in which he'd grown up changed around him. While he has held his ground, the Anglican communion has moved on, increasingly cut loose from its historical anchors in the deposit of faith. Always in his own mind a kind of Catholic, Fuller finally came to the realization that the kind of Catholic he must formally become is the Roman kind. But this was not so much a movement on his part as a dawning recognition.

Let the last word be his: "I don't have an antipathy to the Episcopal Church, and I still have lots of friends there. It's not like I feel some profound distaste or anything like that. It's really much more positive than that, it's just that . . . I use the phrase that [Richard John] Neuhaus used to describe his own movement, which is 'to become the Catholic that you always were.' That's how I'd put it, that I was always what I am, and I've found a place where I can more fully express that."

Chapter Twelve

Studying the Reformation "Turned Me Into a Catholic"

Lucy Beckett

Interviewed by Erika Kidd

Lucy Beckett studied history at Cambridge and is the author of several works of fiction, including *The Leaves are Falling*, *A Postcard from the Volcano*, and *The Time Before You Die: A Novel of the Reformation*, as well as her highly acclaimed work *In the Light of Christ: Writings in the Western Tradition*. She lives in Yorkshire, England, where she taught at Ampleforth Abbey.

Erika Kidd, a convert herself, is Assistant Professor and Director of the Master of Arts in Catholic Studies at the University of St. Thomas in St. Paul, Minnesota. She did her undergraduate degree at Baylor University and graduate work in philosophy at Villanova. She writes on Augustine and the Augustinian tradition.

Erika Kidd: *It's a pleasure to talk with you about your conversion to Roman Catholicism and how that decision has shaped your life, your teaching, and your writing, as an academic and as a novelist. Let's start at the beginning. Please tell us a bit about your childhood experiences of faith.*

Lucy Beckett: My parents were very young. After a hasty

wartime marriage, with my father already a soldier, they were only twenty-three and twenty when I, the oldest of three children, was born. The marriage survived; they had been married fifty-nine years when my mother died. My father died a year later. As a small child I was mostly brought up by an old-fashioned English nanny, who took us children to Sunday school and later to church every week. I always enjoyed this and wasn't bored. My parents were, like most privileged people of their kind at that time in England, nominally members of the Church of England, but apart from baptisms, weddings, and funerals, they never went to church and regarded themselves as agnostics. Really, they were atheists with a sound moral sense derived from Christianity. As a bright, literate fifteen-year-old who read a great deal, I decided that I was an atheist who had understood that God no longer existed and therefore never had existed: I suppose I was establishing to myself that I was cleverer and more advanced than my nanny. At sixteen, however, I must have realized that I needed something more than what seemed obvious: I chose to be confirmed, at my Church of England boarding school, and in the holidays I started going to church by myself early on Sunday mornings, and paying proper attention to the (very fine) Anglican service of Holy Communion.

My parents were surprised but not disapproving. I think they thought this was a phase which would pass, and the Church of England was, after all, familiar and harmless. I was lucky to have the education and the scope to think and read and feel for myself. I knew early on that there were big questions that my parents, who were good, kind, and in most ways supportive, simply ignored or had decided were part of the past and not interesting to them.

My grandmother, a devout Anglican, lived a few miles

away from my family, at Rievaulx, a small Yorkshire village, with a famous and very beautiful ruined Cistercian abbey, destroyed by Henry VIII in the sixteenth century. As a child, I often bicycled to Rievaulx, to visit my grandmother but also to sit among the ruins of the abbey wondering why it affected me so deeply. The existence and the beauty of those ruins—in the village where my husband and I have been fortunate to live for the last forty-five years—were important to me in ways I began to understand only later.

Tell us about some of your best teachers. What role did they play in preparing you for your conversion and sustaining you in your decision?

As a schoolgirl I was taught music, some German and some Greek by a Prussian refugee from Nazi Germany. He was neither a Jew nor a Catholic, but the moral stance represented by his leaving a prosperous life in Germany in protest against Hitler, and his deeply educated European background, were very impressive to a teenager in 1950s England. His story was more or less that of Max in my novel *A Postcard from the Volcano.*

At Cambridge I was lucky enough to be taught by three outstanding scholars. Geoffrey Elton, a Jewish refugee from Germany, was a great scholar of the Tudor period in English history. He was anti-Catholic and dubious about Thomas More. His lifelong work on Thomas Cromwell is unassailable, but his admiration for this wrecker of Catholic England was something I learned quite soon to counter in my own mind. Walter Ullmann, a major authority on the history of the medieval Church and on canon and civil law, was also a Jewish refugee from Hitler, but was a Catholic convert and a wonderful, erudite, warm-hearted teacher. Best of all, Fr. David Knowles, a Benedictine monk and Regius Professor at Cambridge, taught the course on medieval thought, another seminar that I was lucky to be able to join. I read his books and discovered in them the answers to my childish questions about the abbey at Rievaulx, and the full story of the dissolution of the monasteries. My book about the English Reformation is rooted in his account of the Carthusian martyrs.

It was my work, in my first undergraduate year, on the Reformation that showed me what was incoherent and (deliberately) confused in the Church of England, and what turned me into a Catholic. I remember writing an essay on Thomas More and understanding properly that he had died for the unity of the Church, knowing that defying Henry VIII would mean sacrificing his life, and that he was right. At the same time, I was taking a course on medieval thought, which meant Catholic theology from Augustine to fourteenth-century nominalism. This revealed a richness and depth my school education had never suggested. So it soon seemed a natural, and the only sensible, thing to take instruction and ask to be received into the Church.

When I became a Catholic, I had already been a conscious and believing Christian for a couple of years in spite of the scepticism and secularism in almost all of those around me. Deciding to be received into the Catholic Church was the logical and rational thing to do, given what I had learned and was still learning of its history and theology. It was also an emotional commitment to what was ancient and stable. I was just a nineteen-year-old Cambridge student and there was much about the Church that I discovered only later, but the decision seemed entirely right then and has seemed so ever since.

It is interesting your study of the Reformation motivated your conversion, even though you studied under a critic of the Church. Did you learn things about the Reformation many Catholics would not know?

Catholics, unless they have studied the European sixteenth century with some care, are likely to blame the tragic division in the Church entirely on Luther and the more extreme Protestants of the period. In fact, the involvement of the Church with secular power and politics, the corrupt Renaissance papacy, and the behavior of many spoiled and lazy prelates of the period, strengthened the Protestant case against Rome—and prevented an intelligent, penitent response from the Catholic Church soon enough to make the split unnecessary. By the time the Council of Trent eventually began, opened by Cardinal Pole (the hero of my Reformation novel *The Time Before You Die*), it was twenty years too late to mend the breach. So there were grave faults on both sides of the Reformation division, and for Catholics the faults on their own side are perhaps the saddest.

What else were you reading as a student?

I studied English and French literature, Greek and Latin at school. A number of classical texts, particularly Sophocles's *Oresteia*, some of Plato's shorter Dialogues, and Virgil, had in them a sense of transcendence, divinity, the reality of the invisible, which pulled me out of a shallow sense of the secular being all there is. I read some of Pascal's *Pensées*. English poets, particularly Donne, Herbert and Hopkins, pointed me in the direction of Christianity as a serious challenge taken seriously by very intelligent and perceptive people. Shakespeare has been hugely important to me always.

What role did your friends and fellow students play in your conversion?

I had one childhood friend—he became the writer Piers Paul Read—who was, and has remained, a serious Catholic, and is still a friend. He was more of an influence on me than he realized.

When I was provisionally re-baptized and received into the Church in Cambridge at Blackfriars, Piers Read, then a fellow undergraduate, was my sponsor. I went alone to my confirmation a few weeks later in Westminster Cathedral, not telling my parents where I was going. My confirmation sponsor was a stranger assigned to me as the line of perhaps twenty people being confirmed was sorted out.

Otherwise my friends at Cambridge were studying various branches of science, or philosophy, and were startled and shocked by my decision to become a Catholic, a decision they couldn't understand and had no wish to try to understand. Two of my closest friends were secular Jews—I then didn't know that my mother was three-quarters Jewish by descent—and they were particularly shocked: Catholics, they thought, were by definition anti-Semitic.

Were there intellectual or theological barriers to your conversion? Cultural or familial barriers?

There were no intellectual, cultural, or theological barriers: I found, as I have since, every idea or thought I had managed to have falling into place in the Catholic context I was learning about and beginning to experience.

My parents and the wider family, apart from my Anglican grandmother, were, on the other hand, horrified, and did their best to dissuade me. The reasons for their negative reaction were mixed: my mother's liberal, entirely secular family, intelligent and civilized, thought that becoming a Catholic meant abandoning all independence of thought, all freedom to be oneself in one's own way, while my father, a lovely man but an old-fashioned upper-class Englishman, turned out to have a deep prejudice against Catholics as unreliable, foreign, un-British. He couldn't bear the idea of his grandchildren being brought up as Catholics.

This prejudice is still quite widespread in the UK and goes back to the Spanish Armada, the Gunpowder Plot, and centuries of suspicion of France in particular, and scorn for the Irish, the Poles, the Italians. It is one element in the disaster of the Brexit referendum: too many people instinctively feel that Europeans are Catholics and we British don't like them, and it is true that all the founding fathers of the European Union after 1945 were Catholics.

There shouldn't be any tension between being English and being Catholic: England was a Catholic country for twice as long as it has been (officially) Protestant, and there are many Catholic families who preserved the Faith through the centuries of persecution and then adverse discrimination. (Catholics were not allowed to be members of parliament until 1829 or to attend Oxford or Cambridge until the 1870s.) Apart from the disapproval of my father, I personally have never found any difficulty in being Catholic and English—although in the last thirty years British publishers have regarded my books as too Catholic to be likely to do well in the UK.

My father got over it, and loved me and my children in spite of our being papists.

What big questions were you wrestling with at the time of your conversion? Do you still wrestle with them today?

The big question has for me always been the sinfulness and suffering of the world, some of it inflicted by people who think of themselves as devoted to or sanctioned by God. Alas, this has applied to Christians, and does apply to some Muslims, and even, now, to some Israelis and some Buddhists. Trying to keep in balance belief in the mercy of God and belief in the justice of God is never easy, and is harder in the complicated world we live in now than it was when I was young. But Christians must try.

I have never, since becoming a Catholic, felt or thought that God isn't there, here, wherever, or that Christ, who is the meaning of everything, was only a good man who died.

Whom did you choose for your confirmation saint?

I chose Our Lady and have never regretted the choice. When I said to my family I was going to be a Catholic, my nanny said, "You can't do that. Roman Catholics worship the Virgin Mary." This got me inquiring about and discovering actual Catholic teaching and practice in relation to Our Lady, and I have ever since found her presence in Catholic life moving and encouraging. Protestants leave her to one side of the story, so she was almost a new discovery for me, as was, of course, the Rosary, which I have loved ever since.

You converted as a young woman of nineteen. I believe you married young too. What difference has it made to your life and to your faith that you made such weighty commitments as a young woman?

I was converted at nineteen and, still nineteen, married a few months later. The marriage, undertaken far too young and far too impulsively, failed. I was divorced and soon remarried, but I had to cope with thirty years of Catholic life outside the sacraments. I persisted, always went to Mass, and found my faith deepening over the years, so I never once regretted my conversion, and understood the logic of the Church's apparently harsh treatment of the divorced and remarried.

My first husband was nominally a Catholic, so we were sacramentally married in church, but he had really given up the Faith even before we married and as far as I know—we are on friendly terms—has never returned to it. My second husband (we have been married forty-seven years) is an Anglican, not very interested in theology or Christian history, mildly anti-Catholic but tolerant of my Catholic life and work.

Living thirty years as a Catholic apart from the sacraments must have been quite difficult. In light of conversations about divorced and remarried Catholics' reception of the Eucharist, would you say something about the Church's teaching and practice? Do you hope for changes now?

It was difficult, particularly to begin with, to be, as a recent convert, excluded from the sacraments. But I recognized that my first marriage had collapsed largely through my own fault, and that the Church's view of my second marriage as gravely sinful was theologically sound: the sacraments are a coherent system, and to have broken faith with one was, I thought, necessarily to have incurred exclusion from the rest.

Years later, when old age (my husband is fifteen years older than me) had delivered a brother-and-sister relationship, I was allowed to return to the sacraments and this was, of course, a great joy. I hope that parish priests may soon be allowed to take a compassionate pastoral view of individual cases, as we know some do already.

What was your greatest joy in your early months and years of being Catholic?

Feeling at home in the ancient ways of the Church. I was stunned and very much moved by my first experience of the Triduum liturgy. Quite soon after my reception everything changed because of Vatican II, and I was sad to lose the Latin I had recently come to love (and understood because I knew the language). But I was all for the council and have remained hopeful that more of what it recommended will actually happen.

I also much appreciated the mix of people, from all over the world, and the lack of formality—no special clothes for Sundays, nobody minding crying babies or old tramps fast asleep—at any Catholic Mass, so different from the highly respectable atmosphere in the Church of England.

I was surprised and delighted by the warmth of the welcome I was given in the Church. Now, I am still surprised by the strength the Church has given me in facing difficult family problems such as every family has to deal with.

How has being Catholic influenced how and what you teach? What difference has it made to your professional life?

Most of my teaching career was in a Benedictine school, attached to Ampleforth Abbey, so everything I taught (mainly English literature but also some history and Latin and European literature) was done in a Catholic context. The result of those twenty years was my book *In the Light of Christ*, which intended to give senior students in high school, and undergraduates in humanities courses, a

Christian historical and theological context for their study of the great texts of the Western tradition.

After I retired from Ampleforth, I taught Latin for seven years, as a volunteer, in the local state (public) high school, where my students, with few exceptions, had little Christian background, and I made sure that, while studying the language, they also collected some sense of the story of Latin as the binding language of the Church, and of the education of Western Christendom, for so many centuries.

Many converts—such as Augustine—report their conversions followed close on the heels of reading the conversion stories of others. Seeing another's path can help one find one's own. What conversion stories are dear to you?

I hadn't read Augustine when I became a Catholic, though I knew a little about him. Since then, I have read all his big books, the *Confessions* three or four times, and many books about him, and he has become my hero, my favorite saint, almost my friend. I have written about him several times. He presides over my latest novel, not yet published, which is partly set in (modern) Algeria, his country, and which attempts to tell the story of a modern conversion, that of a young man brought up in a secular family with an entirely secular French education.

I've never read another conversion story which comes close to Augustine's. Much later I read about Cardinal Newman's conversion, from the Church of England to the Church of Rome (a slow, intellectual, adult version of my own), and could well understand the mixture of joy and grief that it caused him. In England the established church has all the great cathedrals and beautiful medieval parish churches, all once Catholic, and also all the best music— difficult to leave behind.

Commenting on Augustine's conversion, you write that conversion to Christianity is not an "intellectual conclusion," but "a way of being, a commitment of a life into the hands of God."[4] What way of life have you found within the Catholic Church over the past six decades?

The reality of the Mass and the ancient solidity of the Church, in spite of all its troubles and all its mistakes, were what, most of all, pulled me in and have held me ever since.

---

4   Lucy Beckett, *In the Light of Christ: Writings in the Western Tradition* (San Francisco: Ignatius Press, 2006), 93.

Chapter Thirteen

An Anglican Priest "Plugs In" to the Mystical Body

Michael Ward

Interviewed by Helena M. Tomko

Michael Ward is Senior Research Fellow at Blackfriars Hall, University of Oxford. He is the author of the award-winning *Planet Narnia: The Seven Heavens in the Imagination of C. S. Lewis* and co-editor of *The Cambridge Companion to C. S. Lewis* and *C. S. Lewis at Poets' Corner*. Ward presented the BBC1 television documentary *The Narnia Code* (2009), directed and produced by the BAFTA-winning film-maker Norman Stone, and authored an accompanying book entitled *The Narnia Code: C. S. Lewis and the Secret of the Seven Heavens*.

Previously, Dr. Ward served as Chaplain of St. Peter's College in the University of Oxford and Chaplain of Peterhouse in the University of Cambridge. He was resident Warden of The Kilns, Lewis's Oxford home, from 1996 to 1999.

Helena M. Tomko is assistant professor of literature in the Department of Humanities at Villanova University. She grew up in the Northeast of England, before completing her undergraduate degree in German and Italian at the University of Bristol and her DPhil in German at St. John's College, Oxford University. Her scholarship focuses on German Catholic literature and intellectual culture during the Weimar Republic and Third Reich, as well as on the sacramental vision in Catholic fiction.

Helena Tomko: *The path that you and I took into the Catholic Church shares some similarities. We are both, in a way, "Oxford converts," whose departure from Anglicanism to Rome owes a lot to Oxford's invigorating intellectual and religious life. But this biography is mine only by association. I'm a "rocking horse Catholic," to borrow Caryll Houselander's coinage for someone who is neither a cradle Catholic nor true convert. I was five when my parents left behind late-1970s high Anglicanism, with all its bells, smells, and institutional security. They were received into the Catholic Church in the first year of the pontificate of St. John Paul. I'll never forget our first Catholic Sunday in Oxford, when we walked straight past the pealing bells of our old Anglican church and its liturgical grandeur within, en route to a liturgically sparse, almost makeshift celebration of Holy Mass at the Oxford University Catholic Chaplaincy.*

Like my father, you left Anglican ministry when you entered the Catholic Church in 2012. He was ordained a diocesan priest in 2003, and you'll be ordained soon as a priest of the Personal Ordinariate of Our Lady of Walsingham. But I suspect that this distance of twenty-five years, among other things, makes your path from Anglicanism to Catholicism rather different from the one we trod as a family.

How would you describe the Anglican life that formed you and that drew you toward ordination?

Michael Ward: I was raised in a tradition of Anglicanism which is probably best characterized as conservative evangelical, of the sort associated with John Stott and Inter-Varsity Press. My father and mother were both devout Christians who taught me and my brothers to pray and read the Bible. Family life centered upon the local parish church (in a mid-Sussex village), which had then, and still has today, a large and active congregation. It was fairly

formal and liturgical by the standards of evangelicalism in
the Church of England nowadays, with a careful adherence
to the Book of Common Prayer and to the other written
forms that were coming in then (such as The Alternative
Service Book). We chanted psalms and canticles. I was a
member of the choir, which was robed (with special hats
for the women). But though it was formal in those respects,
it was otherwise "low Church." The vicar and the curate
always wore choir dress (cassock, surplice, preaching scarf,
and academic hood), never chasubles. There was no talk
of the clergy as priests; they were ministers, which meant,
chiefly, ministers of the Word. There was a thriving team
of lay preachers and a strong emphasis upon the sermon
as the center of the service. We didn't use terms like "Eucharist," let alone "Mass": it was Holy Communion or the
Lord's Supper when it happened, which wasn't weekly but
monthly. I have a faint memory of a time when we still
turned east for the Creed, but that was gradually abandoned as a practice. The idea of the Real Presence was
considered mistaken, and there was no tabernacle or re-
served sacrament. The word *sacrament* was hardly ever used.
Children were baptized as infants, but there was a feeling
that the more sacramental aspects of baptism were something we had to accept as members of the Church of England, not because they were key parts of our biblical faith.
We were taught to be wary of ritual, of "churchianity," and
even of "religion": we lived out a faith, we didn't practice
a religion. Evangelism was given a high priority with frequent guest services and special outreach events. Most of
the regular congregation was deeply committed, with lots
of people attending services twice on Sunday, not to mention the midweek home groups for Bible study (my parents
ran one such group). The youth ministry was also large

and vibrant, and I went successively through all its stages: Climbers, Explorers, Pathfinders, Wayfarers. When I went to Oxford, I naturally attended St. Ebbe's, which belonged to the same conservative evangelical stable. And when I was selected for ordination training in the Church of England, I chose to go to Ridley Hall in Cambridge because it was considered both soundly evangelical and intellectually rigorous. Also, knowing Oxford well, as I did by then, I wanted to see what the "other" university was like.

In short, I have much to be thankful for in my upbringing and in the faith formation that I received. I'm more grateful than I can say to my parents for everything they taught me and modeled for me by way of their personal example.

How did you encounter the Catholic Church prior to your decision to enter the Church?

Growing up, I was taught to be quite suspicious of Catholics (and even of Anglo-Catholics). We felt that they *might* be Christians, but if so, it was probably more in spite of their Catholicism than because of it. I popped into Westminster Cathedral once, as a teenager on a visit to London, and found it gloomy and oppressive. I didn't knowingly meet a Catholic until I went up to Oxford. Nonetheless, I was reading J. R. R. Tolkien and G. K. Chesterton from a fairly early age and I liked what they wrote, so I assumed Catholicism couldn't be all bad.

When I finally got to know some living, breathing Catholics, I discovered that they could actually have quite a lively faith. A few of them, even, were possibly holier than I was(!). I didn't understand why the crowds on television went so wild for Pope John Paul II, but I could perceive he was a godly man. I went to hear Mother Teresa when she gave an address at the Oxford Union, and even got to ask her a question at the end of her talk, and it was as plain as a pikestaff that she was aglow with a divine light. But still, I also knew many holy Protestants, so these encounters didn't consciously shift me in a Catholic direction.

The only aspect of Catholicism that I looked upon and consciously admired, and knew that Anglicanism lacked, was clear, coherent teaching on sexual ethics. As soon as I was old enough to understand what abortion and contraception were, I instinctively knew they couldn't be right. And while I was training in Cambridge, I read for the first time papal documents such as *Humanae Vitae* and they made sense to me. The teaching was hard to live out, but it held together. I thought to myself, "These papist chaps have thought about things very thoroughly." But the Church of England was mysteriously quiet on such issues, and that was increasingly a disappointment to me.

Shortly prior to my decision to enter the Church, I struck up a friendship with a recent Catholic convert, David Baird (now a professor at Catholic Pacific College in Canada), who challenged a lot of my Anglican presuppositions. I began attending Mass with him from time to time, and, though I never received Communion, I did have some powerful experiences of the holiness of the Blessed Sacrament, radiating from the tabernacle. One such experience, actually, was at your father's church, St. Gregory and St. Augustine, in Oxford. It was a strange sensation and it lingered overnight. I remember waking up the next morning feeling "plugged in" to the Mystical Body of saints and angels in a new and invigorating way.

As for the decision to swim the Tiber, the proximate cause was a conversation I had with this same friend, David, about the pope. I asked him how submission to the pope differed from submission to the leader of a cult. In becoming a Catholic, wouldn't I be agreeing in advance to anything the pope might say? What if the pope told me, like Jim Jones told his disciples at Jonestown, to drink poisoned Kool-Aid? My friend, rather than dodging the term "cult leader," took it head on and reminded me that *cult* isn't necessarily a dirty word. It just means a form of worship. The Christian cult was established by Jesus Christ with a particular constitution, an apostolic constitution, with Peter and his successors at its head, holding the keys, serving as prime minister to the king. "Whoever receives you receives me," Jesus said, to the Twelve. It is Christ's Church, but his authority is deputed to his apostles, the chief of whom is the holder of the Petrine office, Christ's particular vicar. Now, I had always said that I would follow Christ wherever he led, would obey Christ whatever he required of me, so I was evidently not averse in principle to "agreeing in advance to whatever my cult leader asked." The question I was really struggling with, I began to see, was not about authority as such, but about where that authority, Christ's authority, was located. If it wasn't to be found in a two-thousand-year tradition of magisterial teaching, headed by the pope, where was it? In the General Synod of the Church of England? In my own theological wisdom interpreting "the plain sense of Scripture"? When I put the question to myself in those terms, it became pretty easy to discern where the likeliest answer lay. And not long afterwards I became aware that my ecclesiological fate was a done deal: it was inevitable that I would become a Catholic. The only question was when and where. I had to resign from my position as Chaplain of St. Peter's College, Oxford, and that was a hard decision to take, because it was a very pleasant role—a job I could probably have held for the rest of my career, if I'd wanted to. But

as with Newman realizing he would have to bid farewell
to the beautiful snapdragon outside his Oxford window,
so I came to realize that there were far more important
considerations than my own comfort and security. To cut a
long story short, I was catechized and reconciled with the
Church by your father, Fr. John Saward, at St. Gregory and
St. Augustine's in Oxford, on the Feast of St. Michael and
All Angels in 2012.

*That serendipity makes doing this interview all the more of a
pleasure for me! I'm surprised that we've got this far into our
conversation without you mentioning the writing of C. S. Lewis.
You're one of the leading authorities on this great Christian apol-
ogist, who is at the heart of your extensive scholarship, publishing,
and teaching. Your stumbling upon the hidden celestial code struc-
turing the* Chronicles of Narnia—*which you explain in* Planet
Narnia: The Seven Heavens in the Imagination of C. S.
Lewis *(2010)—is one of the most enviable literary eureka moments I can imagine. Lewis speaks with clarion voice to so many
Christians and seekers. His works are uniquely ecumenical in their
evangelizing warmth and clarity. Now that you are reading him
with, so to speak, Catholic eyes, are you seeing new dimensions—
or new difficulties—in his work?*

Yes, I am beginning to see two particular difficulties. One is
how undeveloped his ecclesiology was, even by Protestant
standards (see *C. S. Lewis and the Church*, edited by Judith
Wolfe and Brendan Wolfe for more on that). The other
is his blind-spot with regard to the Blessed Virgin Mary
(about which Jason Lepojärvi has written illuminatingly in
Religious Studies), a blind-spot one can detect, for instance,
in the fact that, in the *Chronicles of Narnia*, Aslan has no
mother. But despite these difficulties, Lewis remains a great
help in many ways—theologically, ethically, intellectually,

imaginatively—and I continue to study him with deep admiration and gratitude. And I note with pleasure that I am in good company in this regard, for two recent popes have spoken of their high esteem for his writings, John Paul the Great singling out *The Four Loves* and Benedict XVI *The Abolition of Man* for special praise.

The most famous of Oxford converts is Blessed John Henry Newman, who established a precedent for writing about conversion from Anglicanism to Catholicism in his Apologia pro vita sua. *This beautiful testimony could nonetheless disappoint with its itemizing of books read, theological questions posed, and polemics engaged. But this is also true of the religious memoirist par excellence, St. Augustine, whose spiritual autobiography at times also reads as a bibliography of his intellectual conversion. What books and writers would show up in the bibliography of your conversion?*

Yes, I read Newman's *Apologia* about a year before I took the decision described above, and I did find it somewhat disappointing. Newman is quite an acquired taste, I think, and though I have now acquired the taste and find his writings profitable and inspiring, the *Apologia* left me rather nonplussed at the time.

Augustine's *Confessions*, which I first encountered when I was at Ridley, had a more discernible effect in making me view Catholicism positively, but even *Confessions* didn't register with me consciously as a book that was making it likelier I myself would eventually one day cross the Tiber, any more than did the following titles (though I now see, in retrospect, that they were indeed all helping prepare the ground). In no particular order, they include: *The Imitation of Christ* by Thomas à Kempis (a book which I found extremely nourishing and challenging in my teens); *Something Beautiful for God* by Malcolm Muggeridge; Tolkien's

The Lord of the Rings; *Brideshead Revisited* by Evelyn Waugh; parts of *Under the Mercy* by Sheldon Vanauken; and generous helpings of Chesterton, even though some of his books (such as *Orthodoxy* and the early Father Brown volumes) were written before he himself was officially a Catholic. These writers all subliminally warmed me up to Catholicism.

If I were to provide a bibliography of works that made me *consciously* revise my attitude toward and increase my respect for things Catholic, it would be surprisingly short. It was only *Humanae Vitae* and associated texts on sexual ethics that made me think that there was a definite implication here that I would have to wrestle with, ecclesiologically speaking. Ironic, isn't it, how an encyclical that caused great controversy at the time and led so many Catholics to leave or become semi-detached from the Church should have exerted such a powerfully attracting effect upon an outsider like me!

I looked at almost nothing that could be characterized as anti-Anglican or anti-Protestant. If anyone loosened my attachment to the Church of England it was only William Oddie, whose *What Will Happen to God?* and *The Crockford's File* I read with reluctant and dismayed agreement. Mary Loudon's *Revelations: The Clergy Questioned* wasn't written with the intent of loosening the reader's attachment to the Church of England, but I think it did have that effect on me. Of the clergy whom she questioned, only the bishop of London, Graham Leonard, really impressed me as someone who had a definite realization of the supernatural claims of Christianity. And by the time Loudon's book came out, Leonard had become a Catholic, a fact which I knew and which gave me pause for thought.

Newman is reassuringly honest in his Apologia about the diffi-culties he had adopting some Catholic pious practices. I'm forever grateful to the parishioners of the rural parish I grew up in, who made First Holy Communion, Benediction, frequent confession, Stations of the Cross, et cetera seem so simple to me, especially in the early years when my parents were more self-consciously learn-ing the ropes. Do aspects of Catholic piety and devotion still make you scratch your head?

Indulgences! I've heard priests explain them, and I've read apologists defend them, but, however much I try, I still can't quite get my head round what they mean or how they work or why they matter.

Marian devotions were foreign to me when I first swam the Tiber, but they quickly ceased to be alien. Now I not only understand and accept them but find the Marian dimensions of Catholic piety to be extremely helpful. I would put Marian devotions a close third, after daily Mass and frequent confession, in a list of the things I have found most beneficial to my spiritual regimen since becoming a Catholic. But really, it's not just a question of adding things to an existing way of life; it's more like a total transforma-tion, a paradigm shift, as Thomas Kuhn would say.

Any attempt to describe something as definitive as religious con-version runs into the classic conundrums of spiritual writing. Grace is at work, and grace graciously defies description. The novelist Muriel Spark handled this with humor in her short essay "My Conversion." Avoiding sentiment, she says that she never really liked Catholics before she became one and didn't care much for them afterward, just preferable to other people on account of "basic things" shared. I'm not inviting you to say what can't be said about the Holy Spirit's working in your life. But I would like to know whether you have any good jokes about becoming a Catholic?

In the months that led up to my resigning my chaplain's
position at Oxford, the joke was on me—repeatedly. Let
me give you three examples.

First, on the very day that St. Peter's College offered
to make my position permanent, I was driving home and
found myself stuck at traffic-lights behind a bus, on the
back end of which was an advert for Turkish Delight. To
a reader of C. S. Lewis, Turkish Delight can have only one
meaning: temptation. (It's with Turkish Delight that the
White Witch tempts Edmund to betray his siblings in the
first Narnia story.) I chuckled ruefully to myself, as I studied this advert, and took it as a sign that, however attractive
a permanent chaplaincy position would be, I would have
to decline it.

The second example occurred as I conducted my final
service as an Oxford chaplain, towards the end of June
2012. We were marking the Feast Day of St. Peter and I
asked a (rather elderly and frail) don to read the passage
from Matthew's Gospel giving Peter's great confession at
Caesarea Philippi. I didn't know that this aged Fellow had
a glass eye and that he wasn't entirely reliable at the lectern.
He managed successfully to read Jesus's question, "But who
do you say that I am?" His eye then skipped a line and he
omitted to read Peter's answer, "You are the Christ, the son
of the living God." At St. Peter's College, on St. Peter's Day,
St. Peter's great confession of faith was *not* heard!

And this was not the only significant thing about that
service. The guest preacher got up into the pulpit and
was half way through his sermon when we all began to
hear a noise in the street outside the chapel. It got louder
and louder and eventually we realized we were hearing
a Eucharistic hymn sung by a large procession of Catholics parading through the streets of Oxford for the Feast

of Corpus Christi. The preacher calmly said, "I think I'll just pause for a moment while we let them pass." That, I felt, was yet another indication of where the ecclesiological wind was blowing.

And finally, during that summer vacation, I accompanied the chapel choir to Liverpool where they were singing a week's residency in the Anglican cathedral. I had never visited Liverpool before and I was keen to see both the Anglican cathedral and the Catholic cathedral, which stand at opposite ends of Hope Street. I'm told that the Anglican tower is taller, but the Catholic cathedral is built on higher ground.

I drive up to Liverpool and check into my hotel, very keen to nip out as soon as I can in order to see these two buildings. I go up to my room on the third floor and look out the window to check on my car, which I've parked in the hotel car park but in a space which I'm not quite sure is legitimate. I'm worried that I've parked in the wrong place or that I've blocked someone in. I look down on the car park, but all seems in order, so I unpack my bag. Then, still a little worried, I check on the car a second time, but all still seems to be well. Having freshened myself up, I decide to take one last peek at the car, just to make sure it hasn't been towed away or clamped and, this time, when I look out the window, I notice not just my car and the car-park but, looming over both, filling three-quarters of the sky, the Catholic cathedral, "Paddy's Wigwam," as it's often dubbed. I'd been so preoccupied with my own concerns that I'd managed three times to miss the most obvious thing on the horizon.

Chapter Fourteen

Learning to See as God Sees

Erika Bachiochi

Interviewed by Gabrielle Girgis

Erika Bachiochi is a legal scholar at the Ethics and Public Policy Center specializing in Equal Protection jurisprudence, feminist legal theory, Catholic social teaching, and sexual ethics. She is also a Visiting Scholar at Harvard Law School and a Research Fellow at the Abigail Adams Institute in Cambridge, MA.

Her essays have appeared in publications such as the *Harvard Journal of Law and Public Policy*, *Christian Bioethics* (Oxford University), *First Things*, CNN.com, *National Review Online*, *Claremont Review of Books*, SCOTUSblog, and *Public Discourse*. She is the editor of two books, *Women, Sex & the Church: A Case for Catholic Teaching* (Pauline Books & Media, 2010) and *The Cost of "Choice": Women Evaluate the Impact of Abortion* (Encounter Books, 2004). She is a contributor to the Law Professor Blogs Network blog *Mirror of Justice* and serves on the Advisory Council of the Catholic Women's Forum and the Advisory Board of the Susan B. Anthony Birthplace Museum. She co-founded St. Benedict's, a classical Catholic school in Massachusetts where she served as President of the Board from 2013–2015.

Ms. Bachiochi received her BA from Middlebury College, her MA in Theology as a Bradley Fellow at the Institute for the Study of Politics and Religion at Boston College, and her law degree from Boston University School of Law. She is currently working on a book on women's rights.

Gabrielle Girgis is a PhD student in politics at Princeton University. Motivated by a general interest in the fields of political theory, moral philosophy, and religion, her dissertation explores the nature and political-philosophical grounds of religious liberty. Specifically, it investigates the proper basis and scope for this principle as a distinct right of legal protection for religion and conscience. Central to her project is an effort to explain the human and public value of religion and conscience, and to draw moral-legal implications from that account for civil liberties in a pluralist liberal democracy. Before pursuing her PhD at Princeton, she earned a BA in the Program of Liberal Studies from the University of Notre Dame.

Gabrielle Girgis: *You were baptized in the Catholic Church, and even attended CCD as a child. But you came to understand and embrace Catholicism only much later, in your twenties. What role, if any, did faith play in your upbringing?*

Erika Bachiochi: My father and mother married quite young. They were not a match made in heaven—and after having me and then my brother—their marriage was annulled. I was four. My mother quickly remarried and moved us to Maine where I lived until college; my father, who at that point lived several hours away, also remarried. I saw him and his new wife two or three times a year. Apart from my mother and stepfather's fights and my mother's frequent tears, I remember life as fairly ordinary.

I think we went to Mass most Sundays—until my first Communion and then I don't recall going any more. The priest of our local parish, who'd been a family friend, died and there was little impetus, on the part of my mother or stepfather, to return.

The transition from childhood to young adulthood can be especially turbulent in the absence of stable family relationships or a strong faith community. What were some of the hardest challenges —physical, emotional, spiritual—you faced during that period?

As a young child, I was a good student and a very good athlete. I brought an intensity to everything I did, but especially to sports. I was a fierce competitor and competed at a high level as a youth in swimming. But that was before my mother and stepfather's divorce, which took a toll on me, and on my schoolwork and my athletic performance.

When I was thirteen, my stepfather, who I was quite fond of despite his faults, left our home, telling me during a quiet moment that "sometimes people just fall out of love." After a few months, my younger brother also left, to move in with our father. My mother started to date. My reaction was almost immediate. At thirteen, I began acting out in textbook ways.

As thirteen became fourteen and fourteen became fifteen, and I continued to do more of the same, my confident demeanor, scholarly habits—and especially athletic prowess—began to erode. I watched my gifts wither before me: tennis matches were sunk because of apathy, state records in swimming slipped away due to an inability to focus, soccer games spent in sideline self-esteem pep talks with my coach.

In those difficult years, did you ever have a pivotal moment when you realized you needed help?

When I was sixteen, a boy I'd dated—if you can call it that—took his own life. After days of being unable to cry, as if I was not worthy of grieving him, I went to a therapist. My life took a strong turn that day when I cried—and cried for some time, not only about my friend, but my family situation and my own self-destructive behavior.

I began a desperate search to "find myself"—through books on codependence, the "child within," through one and then another self-help recovery group.

My mother was very much the target of my self-righteous fury—and she heard about it quite a bit. There was some truth in my words, to be sure, but without seeing my own part in things, in the troubles of my life, my words of blame only burned; they did not heal. Perhaps it was not surprising then when, against all my objections, my mother up and married a Dutchman more than ten years her junior and moved herself and my younger sister to the Netherlands. Though I felt abandoned, at that point, it just seemed like par for the course, more fodder for my anger. I was happy to see her go.

Did you make connections during that time to any people who remained morally or spiritually influential in your life? Did any of those relationships lay the groundwork for your return to Christianity?

I had begun attending Twelve Step meetings religiously but that was about all that was religious in my life. God to me was Higher Power one day, a goddess the next. I made good friends at the Twelve Step meetings—and though they were in their thirties, forties and fifties and I in my teens, when I was with them I felt safe, I felt okay. We talked a lot of God then, and I began to pray throughout the day, for strength, guidance, and sanity.

When I arrived in small town Vermont for my first days of college, I immediately made my home at the Twelve Step meetings. As a first-year college student—and especially a college athlete—choosing neither to drink nor hook-up was a great detriment to making friends. Though I was surrounded by others my age, loneliness would overcome me in the dorms up on the hill where campus stood, so I made the descent downtown to meetings daily. Yet, still, I was downcast. Peace would be mine during meetings but flee almost as soon as I left those rooms.

I spent most of the summer after my freshman year back in Maine with a friend I had always been deeply fond of. He'd become quite depressed—also the child of a divorce, though much more recent than mine. I longed to offer him some solace, to comfort him with some insight or advice, some little morsel of peace that I had experienced now and again.

But that August, he hanged himself. The guilt and despair I felt after his death were profound. His suicide, with my mother across the Atlantic and my father a stranger to me, sent me into an emotional abyss.

Returning to college at the end of that month for the women's soccer preseason, I remember hoping a truck would run me over so that the darkness would end. Yet, as always, I made my way to the meetings at the bottom of the hill. I was despondent and finally willing to do the work I had to do to let God in, to let God, the divine healer, begin to heal me. I met a strong and sage woman, who took me through the fourth of the twelve steps—a moral inventory of my life. Here I was to list all the resentments I held toward others and my fears, why I had them, and how they'd affected me. When I was through, I was to pray to have God remove my anger and fear, to ask God to help me see things, see the people in my life, differently. In other words, I was to pray to see my past, my relationships, with my mother and father especially, through God's eyes—to see them supernaturally.

After I had completed the fourth step of the process, but before I had been able to see my mother to make my ninth-step amends, I went to a meeting attended by women only. Again, I was very much the youngster there, with the other six or seven women in the room ten to thirty years my senior. The topic moved to motherhood—and some of the women spoke of their struggle to raise their children well, despite their own difficulty just getting through each day.

God spoke to me vividly at that moment. I saw my own mother through God's eyes. She, like these women here, had mothered me while struggling with her own brokenness. Her father had abandoned her when she was four—and she never saw him again; her childhood was difficult, to say the least. At that moment, I saw her as God's beloved daughter who, like me, was wounded and, like me, had acted out of those wounds. The thought that my mother, toward whom I felt so much self-righteous anger, had felt the depths of emotional pain that I'd experienced in those years grieved me. At that moment, I knew the truth of the Lord's Prayer that we prayed at each meeting's end: "forgive us our trespasses as we forgive those who trespass against us." In seeing my mother through God's merciful eyes, I was able to forgive, and in doing so, I was set free.

Though our relationship is no ordinary mother-daughter relationship, by God's grace, it is strong and deep today.

So a near-constant dialogue with God and a new perspective on your difficult past began to guide you toward Christianity. But your faith also grew from philosophical seeds, nurtured by your passion for learning. You were initially attracted to radical feminism and Marxism as a college student at Middlebury. What drew you to those philosophies? In what ways did you eventually come to find them dissatisfying?

When I had arrived at Middlebury, I had sought out the protective confines of the Women's Center on campus. I stopped shaving my legs, put away my skirts and make-up, and turned some of my unease and discontent outward toward radical feminist causes.

Since I was no longer satisfied with the prevailing culture of "sex, drugs, and rock n' roll," a countercultural worldview was something I really craved by the time I got to college. Active and engaged feminists, both in the Women's Center and in the Women's Studies classes in which I enrolled, provided just this: a complex and compelling narrative that even offered reasons for my own inner turmoil, and much else in life that I'd experienced. After all, apart from the tenets of secular feminism, I had yet to encounter any comprehensive worldview that could explain my discomfort in my own body, my mistrust of men, my competitive animosity toward other women. And the feminists on campus were the only ones I'd met who seemed to care more about real life issues like social justice for the poor and gender inequality than about parties and fraternities.

Naturally, the feminists were pro-choice. Thus, early on in college, the pro-choice reflexes I had as a teenager were transformed into pro-choice arguments. This, despite the fact that I had really only supported abortion as an escape hatch for a sexual permissiveness I no longer believed in by the time I arrived at college.

At that point, I began to consider myself a Marxist feminist—and even volunteered one summer for my congressman, Bernie Sanders. His desire to help the poor seemed authentic to me, and I sensed that current politics were not getting to the root of our troubles. But as I studied and prayed (to God "as I understood God"), I began to resist some of what I was learning in my Women's Studies classes. While in my classes feminist principles were tightly linked to the free love philosophy of the sexual revolution, it seemed to me that feminism—at base a quest for women's freedom and equality—was better joined to my own skepticism of the rampant hook-up culture taking shape around me. Why would a woman with a strong sense of self-worth and a drive to do good in the world give away her body to a man who didn't truly know her, didn't cherish her mind, didn't take delight in her heart, was just going to use her, even if she thought she was just using him? There was nothing dignified in this, nothing personally edifying. And I recognized what I saw on the faces of my friends the morning after: a chasing after a respect that was vacuous. I just didn't understand why more women didn't see it the way I did. With characteristic intensity, I kept seeking something more.

You became further disillusioned with these schools of thought when you spent a semester studying in Washington, DC, and working on welfare reform. How did that experience continue to change your thinking on one of the positions you had long found repugnant in Christianity; namely, opposition to abortion?

I did not begin to question my adherence to Marxist feminist tenets until my junior year in college. The chief difficulty I first had with abortion, for instance, concerned the role it played in the lives of poor women—or the role, it seemed to me, that women's groups like the National Organization for Women thought it should play. I had been studying in Washington, DC, during a semester of my junior year and interning with a small think tank that assisted state legislatures in their efforts to reform welfare. As I became more and more immersed in the problems of the poor, especially poor women, I grew more and more disgusted with the argument put forth by abortion advocates that abortion access would help poor women on the road out of poverty. The thought that we, as a nation, would try to solve the problems of the poor by helping them rid themselves of their own children haunted me. It especially offended me that the poor were not among the membership of the elitist women's groups that supposedly spoke for them.

Opposite this widespread view, which was especially prevalent during the Clinton years in debates over welfare reform, sat Harvard Law Professor Mary Ann Glendon's book *Rights Talk*. My politics professor in DC—a man obviously enamored with the Communitarian movement of the 1990s—had assigned Glendon's book to read, alongside books by the likes of Michael Sandel, Amitai Etzioni, and Robert Putnam. Reading Glendon's masterpiece was the first time I'd ever heard articulated the pro-life, prowoman, pro-child, pro-poor alternative (though that of course was not the main purpose of *Rights Talk*). Rather than offer mere legal autonomy (or "privacy") to the pregnant woman in crisis, the right to rid herself of her own child, Glendon suggested that we might actually go out to meet her needs and offer her the counsel, assistance, and support she needed to be able to care for her child. We might even do well to think more deeply about the familial or social conditions that put her in that position in the first place. Glendon's tender and intelligent prose, cast within my wounded and now prayerful and searching heart, opened the same to something new.

Around the same time, my professor invited George Mason Law Professor Helen Alvaré into class, as a speaker in a series of forums on controversial issues. Alvaré was then working for the Catholic Bishops conference and was in class to represent the pro-life position. Though I didn't want to agree with her, her demeanor was so attractive to me that I remember wanting to listen to what she had to say. The pro-choice advocate who came to class the next day was off-putting, even angry. The fact that I still remember how I perceived these two women, without remembering a single argument they made, is a lesson in itself, I think.

Returning to Middlebury College the following autumn, with newly agnostic views on the issue of abortion (and other new ideas too), I changed my major to political science (and dropped women's studies entirely) so that I could continue my study of political philosophy. Though I had gone to Washington a zealous activist, I came away a real student.

So your intellectual development that semester also changed your direction at Middlebury. When you switched your studies to political philosophy, did you encounter any authors or texts that particularly resonated with or attracted you?

As fortune would have it, the Middlebury professors into whose hands I would fall had been students of the great twentieth century political philosopher Leo Strauss. Professor Paul Nelson introduced me to Plato, Aristotle, John Henry Newman, and Michael Oakeshott, among others. An erudite man of great humility, he taught his students to read the texts with both serious care and abundant wonder. Professor Murray Dry, a most gifted teacher, introduced me to the American Founding and constitutional law, two of my enduring loves.

The close study of classic texts of the Western tradition, along with strong religious intuitions that had been growing within, caused an epiphany of sorts regarding the subject of truth. I came to regard what was true about me, about the physical and metaphysical makeup of the universe, about reality, to be more important than what I felt or wanted the truth to be. That is, truth and the findings of reason (and later, of faith) took on a value well above my reputation among friends and family and my desire for esteem and comfort. I began to care more about forming the right questions than having all the answers.

At what point in this trajectory of study (and continued prayer) did you begin to consider Christianity seriously?

My college hosted a symposium on religion during January of that year. I still had very little interest in so-called "organized" religion, but one title caught my eye: the Catholic Worker Movement and Recovery for the Drug Addict. Although still deeply skeptical of Catholicism, I attended the lecture, and afterward, found myself in a rather lively discussion with the speaker. His wisdom was palpable, and it drew me in. He asked if I'd join him for coffee with one of the students who'd brought him to campus. During that conversation, we talked about God's power to heal and God's love for each of us—and I felt deeply alive. As the hour was coming to a close, the other student who was with us asked if I would like to join them at the Newman Club meeting that was to start just then. Newman Club, I was told, was the Catholic student group on campus. My immediate thought was: *Catholic. No thank you.* But the lecturer who I really liked was going, so I went along.

What kept you connected to the school's Catholic community after that first experience of Middlebury's Newman Club?

Sitting and listening to the other students discuss their relationships with God at this meeting was mind-blowing. They talked about pride and humility, reliance on prayer and struggles with fear, all of which I had hungered to talk

about with others my age. Yet interspersed in their conversation were references to sin, to the Church, to Jesus.
These latter concepts were entirely foreign to me—despite
my few years of Sunday school education. So that night, I
got on my knees beside my bed, a habit born of the Twelve
Steps meetings, and I said to God, who at that point I trusted more than anyone else, "So, God, you and I know each
other pretty well now. We're friends, right? So I need to ask:
do you have a Son? The whole idea is totally weird to me,
but if you do, would you let me know?" I still remember
that moment as if it were yesterday.

God answered my prayer in a book and in a friend. The
book was, of course, C. S. Lewis's *Mere Christianity*. Near
the end of the book, Lewis has two back-to-back chapters
on faith. First, he explains, faith is belief; that is, "accepting or regarding as true the doctrines of Christianity." The
second form of faith is the trust one places in God after
realizing one's bankruptcy, realizing that I cannot live on
my own strength, that I cannot be happy by the force of
my own will, that I cannot follow the life God calls me to
simply by trying really hard at it. We have finally attained to
this higher sense of faith, Lewis writes, when we throw in
the towel and say, "God, I cannot do it anymore; you must
do it; please live through me."

I related strongly with the second type of faith, the
recognition that I was powerless over my life and had to
abandon myself to divine providence. This I was doing
every day, again and again. Lewis's first definition, however,
the story of God revealing himself in human history, was
entirely absent from my own understanding of faith up to
that point. I was familiar only with him revealing himself
in *my* history. But if I was to truly know God and love him
as I wanted to, my experience of faith, though vital for

spiritual growth, was simply not enough. I needed to know whether what Christianity proposed to be true about God and about man were actually true.

One of the students who'd been at the Newman Group meeting was also a member of the men's soccer team, so we were acquainted. Josh had some familiarity with Twelve Step programs, and so, over dinner one night, he guided me through Christianity's basic tenets by translating the spiritual experiences I'd had into Christian language, so to speak. Sin, Josh told me, is simply acting in a way that puts distance between us and God; grace, on the other hand, is the outpouring of God's love into our hearts that enables us to act in accordance with God's will. The more he translated for me, the more I understood that in many ways, I already believed much of Christian teaching and didn't even know it.

The semester that followed, I enrolled in a class on the New Testament. I don't know that I'd ever picked up a Bible before that class. I found Jesus the man deeply attractive. He taught with authority things that I'd learned to be true from my life experience. By now, I'd read many of the masters of Eastern religions. But with Jesus, something was different. The Jesus of the Gospels spoke to my heart, calling it, with all its intensity, to get to know him better. I remember it being particularly amusing to the believing Christians in the class that I would continually dispute the professor who, in his penchant for Jesus Seminar type teaching, wanted to discount many of the passages I just knew to teach one or another profound spiritual truth. This, from the feisty young woman who was cutting her teeth on the Scriptures for the very first time.

So what finally prompted your decisive return to Catholicism? After you went to Mass at the local Catholic parish, what further steps did you take to discern whether you had found the true faith?

I had started to check out the (Protestant) churches of my new friends, one by one, to see if any would feed my desire for closer union with God. After coming back from one of those churches one Sunday, feeling a bit frustrated with the lack of connection I felt at any of them, I knelt down by my bed and said to God, "Please show me which church you'd like me to attend." After saying this prayer, in the back of my mind, I added, "But not the Catholic Church." Although I'd already begun to relinquish many of the more radical feminist views that had made the Catholic Church so abhorrent to me, the thought of affirmatively embracing a church whose teaching I had long regarded as oppressive to women did not sit well with me.

But the local parish priest and I had been acquainted as I spent more and more time with the Christian crowd. Father John was deeply interested in questions of political philosophy, which was my course of studies at the time, and so we had much in common. I ran into him one day on campus and point blank asked him, "So why are you Catholic?" He answered, "Because the Catholic Church is the easiest route to heaven."

I would come to learn that by this Father John meant that God, in his great love and affection for us, established the Church on earth to show us the best means to attain intimate union with him. People can find God through other religions and other churches, but through the Catholic Church, especially by way of the sacraments, God comes particularly close to his children; he unites himself with us to strengthen us for life's journey. What I had understood to be the Church's restrictions on freedom—especially in sexual matters—were actually signposts along the way that marked off dangerous territory, that guided our desires away from those things that are always seductively appealing, but are fleeting, distracting—and damaging—so that we could be free to seek the only thing that truly fulfills our desires: union with God.

Once I came to understand the irresistible love God has for each of us—a love whose power I had personally experienced—the nature of my feminism also changed. My desire to work for the benefit of women (and children) did not lessen; I simply began to recognize original and personal sin, and not the patriarchy, as my prime adversary, and self-sacrificing love, rather than legal commands, as the primary vehicle for cultural transformation. Over the years, and with much study and prayer, I would come to see Church teaching on both sex and human dignity as truly liberating and ennobling.

Not unlike the "honeymoon phase" in marriages, the first months (or years) after one's conversion to Catholicism can seem to be a time of extra grace, clarity, and zeal in living out one's commitment to the Church. Were there particular moments or decisions you made soon after embracing the Faith that you might characterize this way?

A visiting professor of political science at Middlebury suggested I go on to graduate study at Boston College with Fr. Ernest Fortin, a learned theologian with unparalleled training in political philosophy as well. Though Fr. Fortin would fall ill and pass away the same year I arrived in Boston, he would still influence me deeply through my brief visits at his bedside, his masterful writings, and the cadre of impressive students he'd left behind.

As I studied Augustine and Thomas Aquinas, and other early Fathers of the Church, I became more and more drawn to prayer before the Blessed Sacrament. Not knowing if my vocation was to marriage, or single or religious life, I asked Jesus each day to keep my heart with all its burgeoning desire, safe, with him, in the tabernacle of the beautiful stone chapel of St. Mary's at BC.

Realizing my heart still needed healing and having learned how very important fathers are in the healthy upbringing of young women, I asked God, the Father, to re-parent me, to be the father I never really had. And God answered my prayer. First, he afforded me time, as an adult, with my own father, who I came to admire and cherish, because of his great strength, manliness, and spirit of sacrifice for the needs of others. As a grown woman, I was given a taste of the relationship with a father—my father—that I had lacked as a child. I was able to witness his loyalty to and love for his wife, my step-mother; their marriage, based on mutual respect and friendship, became an important example to me. Second, God put in my life good men who were unavailable to me romantically with whom I could build deep friendships—without slipping into the bad habits of my past. And then, God asked me to give up men.

No, I don't mean permanently, but just for Lent. When I told my spiritual director at the time that I was giving up men for Lent, giving up dating them, obsessing over them, flirting with them, for a short six weeks, she asked, "But Erika, what if you meet a handsome, intelligent, funny Catholic man during Lent?" I responded, "Such a man would just have to wait."

Three days before Lent that year, I met the man who would become my husband. And he did wait. A friendship that began over the phone—that is all that I'd allow—grew into a beautiful courtship, and then a happy marriage that has sustained me for the last seventeen years. Our seven lively children have expanded my heart, little by little, offering delights and life lessons that continue to amaze me.

What gratitude I have that in God's mercy and goodness, he has brought so much peace and joy out of such unlikely beginnings!

Chapter Fifteen

Brought to Rome by the Sacrificial Theology of Augustine

Chad C. Pecknold

Interviewed by Matthew J. Franck

Chad Pecknold received his PhD from the University of Cambridge (UK) and since 2008 he has been a Professor of Historical & Systematic Theology in the School of Theology at the Catholic University of America. He teaches in the areas of fundamental theology, Christian anthropology, and political theology. He is the author of a number of scholarly articles and books including, most recently, *Christianity and Politics: A Brief Guide to the History* and *The T&T Clark Companion to Augustine and Modern Theology*. Pecknold is also a frequent contributor to debates in the public square, writing regular columns for *First Things* and *National Review* and has appeared as an invited guest on radio and television shows such as NPR's "All Things Considered," Vatican Radio, Al Jazeera America, BBC World News, ABC News, FOX News, CNBC Squawk Box, and he is a regular contributor on EWTN News Nightly offering his clear analysis and expert opinion on the Catholic Church, the papacy, and the relationship between the Church and politics in American culture.

Matthew J. Franck is Associate Director of the James Madison Program and Lecturer in Politics at Princeton University, Senior Fellow at the Witherspoon Institute, where he directs the Simon Center on Religion and the Constitution, and Professor Emeritus of Political

Science at Radford University, where he chaired the department and taught courses in political philosophy, constitutional law, and American politics. He has written, edited, or contributed to books published by the University Press of Kansas, Lexington Books, Oxford University Press, and Cambridge University Press, and has published articles and reviews in *American Political Thought*, the *Review of Politics*, the *Journal of Church and State*, the *Catholic Social Science Review*, *National Affairs*, *The New Atlantis*, *First Things*, the *Weekly Standard*, the *Claremont Review of Books*, *National Review*, and *Public Discourse*.

A native of Seattle, Washington, Chad Pecknold is associate professor of systematic theology at the Catholic University of America in Washington, DC, where he has taught since 2008. Pecknold's early childhood might be described as a difficult one—his father battling cancer, his mother unable to care for him, and his grandparents taking over until he was about six years old—yet he is very matter-of-fact about it. But then his father "miraculously recovered," his sister (his only sibling) was born, his grandparents moved to California, and his parents were able to stabilize the Pecknold family themselves.

What he remembers of religion in his childhood is—not much. Christmas was "a big deal," as were Sunday dinners. But why Sunday, why Christmas? These seem in retrospect to have been mere "residuals" of Christian life. His grandmother was a "very Catholic Quebecois" woman, and his grandfather, with a Church of Ireland background, agreed to raising their children Catholic. But as for the home his own parents made, "While we sometimes went to my mother's Presbyterian church for Easter, and I sometimes would go with evangelical neighbors to Vacation Bible School, Christian faith was not integral to our life as a family. It was a 'nice' thing, but not a necessary thing. So while it was not an entirely secular upbringing, neither can I call it Christian."

Pecknold's encounter with the call of a Christian life came in his teen years. He had attended a magnet humanities school in Seattle, where a teacher introduced him to existentialists like Camus and behaviorists like B. F. Skinner. From Camus's *Myth of Sisyphus* he took away the message that life "is all meaningless, all I have is my friendships here, that is it." And so one day in his teens, after a relationship with a girlfriend had broken up, he was suddenly struck, while driving somewhere, with the insignificance of our lives "on this tiny blue planet," and he had to pull the car over, simply shaking with the despair of it. What had struck him as the cause of our insignificance was the fact, as he then thought, that there is no god; what made him shudder physically at the thought, "in retrospect," is that "I must have had a nascent, unspoken, naïve implicit faith that there *was* a God."

It was shortly after that, in the darkness of his bedroom in his family's home, that Pecknold literally had a vision. "The room was illuminated, and the face of Christ came to me and said, 'give me your life.'

"I wasn't unaware of Christianity, but I wasn't reading the Bible, I wasn't going to church . . . and I had a vision. . . . I think the face of Christ was very much like Eastern Orthodox icons, it was like an iconic face of Christ. 'Give me your life,' it's all he said. 'Okay! I have no idea what this means,'" he remembers thinking. But "I have been trying to do what he told me ever since, sometimes unsuccessfully."

Pecknold began to attend meetings of Young Life, a network of evangelical Christian clubs for high schoolers. The leader at his school urged him to attend Seattle Pacific University, an evangelical institution founded by the Free Methodists. Immediately Pecknold was drawn to theology classes. At SPU he encountered the countercultural side of evangelical Christianity, reading Stanley Hauerwas and William Willimon's *Resident Aliens* and thinking, "Oh, this is how it is . . . we're set apart, we're in contrast to the culture."

A New Testament professor at SPU named William Lane became a kind of mentor, around whom a group gathered of "about six of us who would meet every week, just to talk, read the Bible together, pray together."

Sunday was "Glory Day" for this group of young men. Pecknold describes the day:

> After chapel, we'd meet to talk, get some breakfast, then go hear Earl Palmer, who was a Presbyterian pastor at the University [Prebyterian] church [near the University of Washington campus]. He was a great preacher. . . . That's when I first realized that being Reformed was about preaching. It's about going to hear the preacher; the preacher's the thing. Then we'd go for a big long hike, or do something big in the afternoon, and then we'd go to St. Mark's [Episcopal] Cathedral for Compline. It was very high church, but socially liberal, and attracted tons of young people who were totally unchurched. You'd go there right about dusk, and you'd see people spread out all over, people you don't normally see in church, and it would be totally dark, and then these men dressed as Anglican monks would come out with candles and chant the psalms.
>
> This looked more like what I'd glimpsed in the face of Christ—more ancient, more profound, not

emotivist. My whole SPU experience was emotivism, small groups, sharing, caring. . . .

And the St. Mark's experience was not about the
preacher, it wasn't about the discipleship group, it was
about hearing the words of Christ chanted in the
psalms that were ancient, that were ever true, that
were profound.

There was something about that Compline experience that was the beginning of a journey. . . . I first
got a glimpse that there was something the face of
Christ was sending me to that was deeper, richer than
the small kind of evangelical subculture I'd discovered.

Pecknold marked another milestone in his journey with
his discovery in a used bookstore of an anthology edited by
Vernon Bourke titled *The Essential Augustine*. He was drawn
into the life and work of the bishop of Hippo immediately.
"It sent me back to the original texts. . . . And it sent me
back to the Bible, and to taking Bible classes. I couldn't
believe that Augustine thought you had to memorize the
Bible. He thinks that every Christian should memorize the
Bible. I thought, oh my gosh, I have to memorize the Bible.
How on earth am I going to do that? And of course, I
didn't, but it did make me read the whole Bible, and I took
as many Bible courses as I could."

Those Earl Palmer sermons at University Presbyterian
Church, often invoking Karl Barth, Dietrich Bonhoeffer,
and C. S. Lewis, had their effect as well. Bonhoeffer's mar-
tyrdom made him realize "I've been called to give my life
. . . and I might have to give it ultimately." And Pecknold
"became a huge C. S. Lewis fan." Lewis "ignited for me the
power of writing, and of being someone who defends the

faith in a winsome way." But his studies took a more patristic turn. And "Augustine was the greatest Church Father
for me."

Pecknold was still in search of what "give me your life"
meant "in concrete terms," and he was uncertain what to
do after college. Earl Palmer suggested Princeton Theological Seminary. But PTS, although it admitted non-
Presbyterian students like Pecknold, did not feel like a good
fit for him, and he left after a year.

A new president at Seattle Pacific University, Philip
Eaton, invited him to return to work on his staff, assigning
him to organize and administer a symposium on Christian
higher education. This was also when Chad met his future
wife, Sara, then a student at SPU. She had been raised in the
Nazarene Church in Kansas, and when Pecknold met her,
"she was deeply informed, as far as an evangelical can be, by
angry feminism." He thought as he courted her, "We'll fix
this," but it was she who turned out to call the tune. Sara
was attracted to Catholicism even before Chad was, but
she was first drawn to Anglicanism; "It was her lead that we
were married in an Anglican church" in 1998.

Pecknold's sojourn at SPU on President Eaton's staff was
brief. One of the people he met there was Lloyd Ogilvie,
then the US Senate's chaplain, who called Pecknold and
asked him to come to Washington to work for him. Pecknold took the job—meanwhile courting Sara from afar and
flying her to Washington whenever he could—but he was
restless and unsatisfied with the work on Capitol Hill. Sara
convinced him to return to grad school, and they moved
after their marriage to California, where he earned his master's degree at Fuller Theological Seminary. Two professors
there in particular, Colin Brown and James McClendon,
urged him to go to Cambridge for the doctorate, under

John Milbank. Pecknold was offered admission to Cambridge, but by the time he and Sara arrived in England, Milbank had left Cambridge for the University of Virginia. At Cambridge, Pecknold wound up studying chiefly under David Ford and Janet Soskice. He intended to write on Augustine's thought on the Trinity. Recoiling from the "social trinitarians" who insisted on "using" the Trinity for this or that purpose, Pecknold wrote a paper on how Augustine used it—anagogically, "to raise you up to worship and understanding of the triune God." This became his first published article, in the *Anglican Theological Review.*

Pecknold was thrilled at this first publication. But "it was almost like I had done the whole dissertation I wanted to do, in the article. . . . And I froze. It was almost like I couldn't go any further with it. That was supposed to become a whole dissertation!"

David Ford, on the other hand, didn't seem worried, pointing his student toward the "Yale school" and the thought of its leading figure, George Lindbeck, who had been a Lutheran observer at the Second Vatican Council. Ford also suggested examining the work of the Jewish philosopher Peter Ochs on the thought of Charles Peirce on the logic of Scripture. These seemingly disparate strands— Augustine, Lindbeck on language and the coherence of tradition, Ochs on Peirce and Scripture—all worked their way into his dissertation. Pecknold began to perceive a difference between what he called "A reasoning," contained in the ancient deposit of faith, and "B reasoning," the work of theologians who strove for a kind of "coherentism" that cannot get out of the "immanent frame."

What we need, he began to think, was "some way of thinking about the Church that had reference to a reasoning that would help it to deepen, to develop, to grow." All unaware as yet, "I was on [John Henry] Newman's road to the development of doctrine, the key to Newman's conversion." Newman was a figure who at first seemed "a fellow Anglo-Catholic who I thought had made a wrong turn . . . but then I saw he had made the only turn he could make." We need "an attachment to a transcendent source of life, to not only Christ's revelation but how it's been developed in continuity through a divine institution, with popes and councils."

The turn toward Catholicism was not as sudden as that, however. In the meantime, the Pecknolds were worshipping in a very Anglo-Catholic branch of the Church of England. But Chad kept coming back to the question of ecclesiology as primary, and with it the apostolic succession, which "mattered as something that God established to guard the deposit," something he did not see the Church of England doing.

If the Church was indefectible, he increasingly thought, then somehow the papacy was too. "Papal claims are just extensions of ecclesial claims. . . . If we want a really coherent Church, it has to have recourse to transcendent claims that govern it, and that has to be Scripture and Tradition, and they have to be juridically enshrined and protected, and that has to be through councils and it has to be through popes, because those are the divine vehicles through which God governs."

He kept these considerations out of his dissertation, forging ahead with writing what he had planned to write, all the while increasingly thinking "we have to become Catholic."

"It wasn't just a metaphysical realism I needed, it wasn't even a theological realism about God that was the most important, but a kind of realism about the Church. So my first conversion was to Christ, and my second conversion was to the true Church, the Church that really communicates the Incarnation."

And his wife? "She was all 'let's become Catholic!' and I'm all cautious, just the way I am with my life: 'I don't know, maybe,'" he says in a plaintive tone to imitate how he felt at the time. Sara was the more eager enthusiast.

Now Augustine entered the picture once again in a decisive way. When he finished the PhD, Cambridge gave Pecknold a research fellowship enabling him to stay for three more years. He decided to go back to Augustine and read *The City of God*. He'd never read it in full before, though he loved Augustine. He gathered some students for a reading seminar and they read it all from start to finish.

Before this, Pecknold had always had a "Protestant Augustine" in view, but now "it was a different kind of text, all built around sacrifice." Most of the reformers of the sixteenth century, Augustinians in their own way, "are happy with the real presence of Christ" in the Eucharist, but "not one of them will accept the view of the Eucharist as sacrifice." Luther, Zwingli, Calvin—for them "that's papist, to think of the Eucharist as sacrifice. Christ's is the one sufficient sacrifice; the Eucharist is not the sacrifice. That's what *Catholics* think."

"This is where I discovered the Catholic Augustine. . . . How do you make sense of *The City of God*? It's about sacrifice." Augustine considers sacrifice in many contexts, including the pagan, but "the true and proper ordering of the suffering of one's life is to the sacrifice of Christ on the cross *and in the sacrament of the altar*. And how does *The City of God* end, but with the martyrs whose names are repeated at the sacrament of the altar, because their lives are conformed to the sacrament." Today Pecknold is at work on a book arguing for the centrality of sacrifice as the organizing principle of Augustine's *City of God*.

But it was in that Cambridge reading group that "I realized Augustine's Catholic. And when I realized Augustine's Catholic, I came home and said to Sara, okay, we're going to be Catholic, because Augustine's Catholic."

At the same time, he was "looking at Augustinians in the Church like Ratzinger being elevated to the papacy. I immediately recognized Ratzinger as a truly Augustinian theologian. I saw him elevated to pope, and I thought, 'Augustine could have been pope!' There's no reason that Augustine couldn't have been."

Stanley Hauerwas, whom Pecknold had come to know, knew that he was leading this little Augustine group at Cambridge, and noticed that Loyola University in Baltimore was using *The City of God* as its common text the next year in a core text program. Hauerwas contacted Loyola and said, "Hire Pecknold; he knows *The City of God*." Chad laughs at this memory and says, "Of course, I'd just read it!" But Augustine's *magnum opus* since then has taken center stage in his teaching and his scholarship.

The Pecknolds returned to the US so Chad could take the job Loyola had offered. As soon as they arrived in Baltimore, the Pecknolds started RCIA in a local Maryland parish and were received into the Church in 2007.

Pecknold's "next conversion" was "praying about my next move." He was not tenure-track at Loyola, but the university had hoped to get him on a tenure-track line after three years. He applied for two jobs in 2007–08, one of them at the Catholic University of America. He learned he was a finalist for both jobs. Not sure whether he would get an offer from either school but wondering if he might get offers from both, he went into Loyola's Memorial Chapel to pray.

Though now a Catholic, Pecknold had no personal Marian devotion at this time. "I knew that Catholics had a devotion to Mary, and I knew theologically in my head why Mary mattered. I could even tell you things that were important about the doctrine of the Immaculate Conception. I could tell you various things, I could probably teach a course." But as for a personal Marianism, "I didn't understand that."

Yet when he went into Memorial Chapel and approached the shrine to Mary to pray about the two jobs, suddenly he felt that the eyes of the icon of Mary were on him, staying with him as he moved. He knelt down, prayed the Hail Mary, and asked for Our Lady's help and guidance, whatever offers might come.

"And it was very, very much like the 'give me your life' moment. She stared me right in the eye, pierced me with her eye, and said, 'I want you to go to Catholic University.' And that was before I got the offer." From that moment forward, Pecknold felt his vocation as a theologian was consecrated to Mary, the Seat of Wisdom.

CUA made him an offer, which he accepted immediately, withdrawing from the other job search without ever knowing if he would be made an offer. More importantly, he had had a conversion to Mary as well, to whom his work was henceforth consecrated.

Chad and Sara Pecknold have been at Catholic University ever since, where Sara is now a professor of music, having earned her PhD at CUA after Chad began teaching there in the School of Theology.

Chapter Sixteen

An Evangelical Seminarian and the Fullness of Faith

Douglas M. Beaumont

Interviewed by R. J. Snell

Douglas M. Beaumont has a PhD in theology from North-West University and an MA in apologetics from Southern Evangelical Seminary, where he served as assistant to President Norman Geisler and taught Bible and religion for many years. He is the author of *Evangelical Exodus: Evangelical Seminarians and Their Paths to Rome, The Message Behind the Movie,* and has contributed to *The Best Catholic Writing, The Apologetics Study Bible for Students,* and the *Christian Apologetics Journal.* He lives in California with his wife and four children.

R. J. Snell directs the Center on the University and Intellectual Life at the Witherspoon Institute in Princeton, NJ. Prior to this appointment, he was for many years Professor of Philosophy and Director of the Philosophy Program at Eastern University and the Templeton Honors College, where he founded and directed the Agora Institute for Civic Virtue and the Common Good. A convert to Catholicism, he grew up Baptist and received his early education at the schools of Prairie Bible Institute and Liberty University. His first encounter with Rome occurred while pursuing an MA in philosophy at Boston College, where he took several courses with Peter Kreeft. Later he earned a PhD in philosophy at Marquette University. He is the author of several books as well as articles, chapters, and essays in a variety of scholarly and popular venues. He and his family reside in the Princeton area.

R. J. Snell: *In* Evangelical Exodus, *you note that while it's not technically correct to describe a validly baptized Christian as "converting" when they enter into full communion with the Church, you use the term, in part, because "becoming Catholic is, for an Evangelical, nearly as dramatic as that of a pagan." But you also say that Evangelicals do not "relinquish" their belief so much as "receive" faith when they convert. A cradle Catholic might not understand why the experience is so markedly dramatic but not an abandonment of earlier faith—would you explain a bit more?*

Douglas Beaumont: Many "cradle Catholics" do not grasp how much the Church is vilified by many non-Catholic Christians. They generally see these communities as merely lacking in some graces, or wrong on a couple issues, but otherwise generally "Christian." What Catholics often don't realize is that the feeling is rarely mutual. Whether it is some Reformed denomination that sees the papacy as the antichrist, or Seventh-day Adventists who think Sunday worship is the mark of the beast, or Fundamentalist Baptists who teach that the Catholic Church is the whore of Babylon, non-Catholic Christians generally take a very low view of Catholics, if not outright animosity. So while a Methodist might become Presbyterian, or a Baptist become Pentecostal, without raising more than an eyebrow or two, a non-Catholic becoming Catholic is often seen as nothing less than apostasy. The irony is that there exists far more difference in both faith and morals between a conservative Protestant and a liberal Protestant than with the Catholic Church! The result is that a faithful Evangelical can find in Catholicism a deepening or expansion of their faith that makes the doctrinal differences less important. But for those who do not see them as additions

to faith, those differences retain the appearance of being
essential truths that are being given up.

*Prior to your interest in Catholicism, what was your perception
of the Church? Were you indifferent, or did you have strong sentiments against Catholicism? How did you get past those sentiments to even begin to take the Church seriously as an option?*

I had strong sentiments against Catholicism, but they were
largely second hand. The vast majority of what I knew and
felt about Catholicism was inherited from an Evangelical
culture that I reflected more than absorbed. Catholicism
was not something I spent very much time thinking about
unless it came up, and it usually did not come up except in
adversarial contexts where I would default to the opinions
and attitudes I found in the books I read. Mea culpa. When
I started to dig into the subject for myself, I rarely found
anything terribly upsetting, and the things I took issue
with I could keep at a respectable emotional distance long
enough to make a more objective intellectual assessment.
The more I learned about true Catholicism, the more I
saw principled analogs in the Evangelical Protestant faith,
shared foundations that simply diverged in application. For
example, immoral popes were no more of a problem than
was St. Peter. The evil of Israel no more made it cease to
be the people of God than evils committed by those in the
Church made it cease to be the Church. These discoveries
made me realize that often it was only my inconsistent application of shared principles that made Catholicism seem
as far off as I had been led to believe it was. After that, the
evident strengths of the Catholic position were far easier
to focus on.

Your road home was influenced by the study of St. Thomas Aqui-
nas while at Southern Evangelical Seminary. Other than simple
exposure to a thinker so important to Catholics, what did Aquinas
provide that moved you to consider Rome? Also, could you provide
some context on why (or if) it is unusual for Evangelicals to study
Aquinas?

In my experience it is unusual for Evangelicals to study
anyone outside their theological bubble. There is, ironically,
a kind of evolutionary view of theology that sees the present as the pinnacle, and old musty writings unhelpful to the
faith. There is also a high degree of reliance on the Holy
Spirit to provide up-to-the-minute guidance in many areas
of life including interpretation and moral decision making.
The Evangelical has his Bible and the Spirit, what else is
required? So it can be seen as sort of a waste of time to
get deep into history—much less *Catholic* history! (For example, Church History was not even taught at Southern
Evangelical Seminary for any graduate level degree, even
as an elective.)

Personally, I found Aquinas to be a brilliant philosopher,
and extremely helpful in apologetics. (This was Norman
Geisler's influence.) Aquinas was such a careful, systematic thinker; it really resonated with me. His theology of
God was amazing, and I found it far superior to the more
pop-theology I was reading from contemporary writers.
One pivotal moment for me was Aquinas's discussion of
heresy. He argues that a heretic lacks faith in even those
doctrines with which he agrees with the Church because
his disagreement shows that he did not have faith in God's
revelation via the Church in the first place. That was a
punch to the stomach—for I had been taught (and had
taught) the very opposite (as all Protestants must). That

haunted me until I came into full communion with the Church.

Please tell us a bit about Geisler. Why was he interested in teaching Aquinas? There are plenty of other Christian thinkers who are helpful for apologetics, so why did Professor Geisler rely on him, especially if reading Aquinas resulted in students becoming interested in Rome? What did Geisler have you read in Aquinas? I assume it was more than the Five Ways which argue for the existence of God—did you study the entire metaphysical and moral framework of Aquinas? What was most unexpected for you when you began to read Thomas?

Dr. Geisler grew up in something of a Catholic culture and was educated at a Jesuit university (Loyola). In his studies, he came across the philosophical school of Thomism and applied it to his apologetic method. Geisler's apologetic is "classical" in the sense that rather than beginning with the Bible or the Resurrection, his "starting line" was the existence of God—and Thomism gave immense metaphysical support to theism. So at the seminary, Geisler had us reading Aquinas's more philosophical works and anything he thought would uphold our basic theology. Depending on the class, we might read these only, but in some classes we read material Geisler disagreed with as well. The most shocked I ever found myself reading Aquinas was definitely his discussion of faith in the *Summa Theologiæ* (II-II Q.5 A.3). He asks if heretics, who deny the faith in some parts have faith in the parts they do not deny. For a Protestant the answer was clearly yes—it seemed silly to even ask. Aquinas's answer was "No." In a nutshell, the reason is that because faith is submission to a religious authority, someone denying what a religious authority teaches cannot be doing so in faith, and this shows that their reason for believing other teachings is not truly by faith either. This amazed and terrified me.

For Catholic theology, tradition and Church history are vitally important, whereas you suggest that the "historic faith" that Southern Evangelical Seminary wished to defend was anything but historic. Could you give some examples of this problem? Also, when you began reading Church history and Church Fathers, what was most startling, unexpected, and problematic for you?

It's hard not to quote Newman here, so I'll just give in: "To be deep in history is to cease to be Protestant." I discovered this through several clues during my time at SES. The first was when I was working with Dr. Geisler on his *Systematic Theology* (vols. 2 and 4). My job was to locate quotes from the Church Fathers that supported his beliefs. This was relatively easy in volume 2 which dealt with God, but in volume 4 (*Church and Last Things*), I had a very difficult time finding anything that sounded plausible. Once I learned more history such as canon formation and orthodoxy development, I realized that some of Dr. Geisler's distinguishing beliefs were not "historic" in the meaningful sense such a claim seemed to convey. The SES doctrinal statement, for example, contains numerous doctrines that only came into popularity during or after the Reformation; others are as late as the nineteenth or twentieth centuries, and many are merely choices from among several historic options. My issue was not whether Geisler's views were wrong, it is that he claimed to defend "the historic faith" of a two-thousand-year-old Church while affirming late doctrinal innovations. To make this claim when his views are clearly in the minority (both historically and presently) seems misleading.

Many converts resonate with the Newman quote you mentioned, but clearly, it's not persuasive to many Protestants. How would well-trained scholars of good will, such as Professor Geisler himself, respond to what you've just stated? What are their strongest arguments? Or, when you were exploring these matters for yourself, what were the arguments that seemed strongest to you at the time?

One response I was taught to this claim was (literally) that old can be gold but it can also be mold, and new can be true. The Church's history, I was told, reveals ongoing development which is sometimes good and sometimes bad. Therefore, age cannot be used to determine truth. But Newman's point is not simply that Catholicism is older than Protestantism. Rather, what history reveals is that Protestantism simply did not exist for the first 1,400 years after Jesus started his Church. What follows is that Protestantism isn't the Church Jesus started. That claim is not answered by an appeal to developmental issues. Further, we find specifically Catholic teachings in the very earliest Christian writings which were composed long before doctrinal development could be credibly blamed for error. Another tactic used by Evangelical scholars such as Geisler is to point out that Eastern Orthodoxy is older than Roman Catholicism because Christianity began in the East, not the West. This is a misleading semantical argument—both Roman Catholicism and Eastern Orthodoxy began, in a sense, at the same time when the one, holy, catholic, and apostolic Church divided in schism. At best this argument simply proves that today's Christian has two options (neither of them Protestant) for entering the historic Christian Church. Other arguments simply begged the question by equating apostolic teachings with the biblical interpretations of whatever group stood in opposition to Catholicism. (See Geisler and Betancourt's book *Is Rome the True Church*. Note that shortly after this book's publication, Joshua Betancourt came into full communion with the Catholic Church!)

Much of your story revolves around the search for doctrinal unity and authority, but you also describe the "functional Gnosticism" of much Protestant worship and its "between-the-ears activity." Could you explain what you mean by that? What role did liturgy or the embodied traditions of Catholic piety play in your conversion, or even your long delay in converting?

The idea of "functional Gnosticism" was introduced to me by my Anglican priest and it struck a chord with me. Basically, I was starting to understand the sacramental view of the world in contrast to the Baptist/Evangelical theology I had been taught. In that system, baptism is just a symbol, communion is just a memorial, secular marriage only differs by degree from Christianity, there is no distinct priesthood, et cetera. Faith was what one affirmed, the statements one agreed with. What mattered for salvation, then, was what one thought was true; it had very little to do with what one did or how one interacted with the world. The physical world was presented as merely our "temporary home" and our bodies as "earth suits" for our souls. Given this backdrop, it's not hard to imagine how bizarre a traditional liturgy seemed! But I have to admit; I loved it. It felt real; my religious beliefs concerning creation were finally making sense with my religious actions. So, although I spent decades in churches with almost no décor (much less statues, icons, candles, or vestments!), the liturgical elements (pun intended) were never a problem for me.

What do you mean by "the sacramental view of the world"? Do you mean the sacraments themselves or something broader? I know

many readers of C. S. Lewis and Tolkien who talk about a sacra-
mental view of the world even if they do not maintain the Catholic
understanding of baptism and the Eucharist, for instance. They
tend to mean something like an enchanted view of the cosmos rath-
er than the flattened, dead mechanism of the modern understand-
ing. Is that what you mean? What would you say to my friends
who have a "sacramental view of the world" but don't accept the
sacraments?

By "sacramental" here I do mean that physical objects are
not simply reducible to matter, that there is an immaterial
component (e.g., "spirit," "soul," "form," etc.) that accounts
for what something is. Thus, what we do with the material
world has implications beyond what is affected by physical laws. Sacraments proper are conveyors of God's grace,
and not everything has that capacity in this strict sense, so
I don't necessarily see it being contrary to reason to hold
a generally "sacramental" view of the world while rejecting specific sacramental theology. I do, however, think that
it can help someone to move along the continuum. So,
for example, a Baptist with a merely memorial/symboli-
cal view of sacramental practices might have a better time
understanding sacramental theology if he comes to see that
his world is "sacramental" in the general sense I am using
it here. For example, many Baptists would be upset over a
flag burning even though a flag is "just" a national symbol.
And even iconoclasts sometimes kiss pictures of their relatives. Once someone acknowledges that there is more to
physical reality than the material, the door is open to move
into more depth.

When young, you "accepted Jesus into your heart," but indi-
cate that a lack of ongoing discipleship, catechesis, and fellowship
"threatened to shipwreck your faith, and you essentially became

agnostic for some time." However, in my experience, Evangelicals often provide more discipleship and fellowship for the young than Catholics do, and many Evangelicals use this lack to critique the Church and argue for Evangelicalism. What are your thoughts on this?

I was not raised in a religious environment. We did not attend church anywhere or read the Bible. I said nighttime prayers with my mom and she would take me to Vacation Bible School some summers though, and it was there that I accepted Christ into my heart (along with my best friend, who is also Catholic now!). However, between that and my eighteenth year there was simply no "input" as far as faith went. So it was not a lack in Evangelicalism, it was that I was simply not a part of it. Once I was in college, I really began my faith life, though, and there I had numerous opportunities and grew in my faith quickly.

Still, I'm sure you're familiar with the criticism about Catholic formation raised by Evangelicals; namely, that Evangelicals, in their own way, tend to be fairly serious about passing on the faith and tackling the hard aspects of sanctification or growing in holiness. When I converted, one of the most frequent questions I received from Protestant friends was precisely about this issue. What are your thoughts about it, especially now that you've been Catholic for a while?

First, I hope I made it clear that my lack of discipleship and fellowship was my own fault. I in no way blame Evangelicalism in general, nor any of the particular groups I came in contact with for my lack of participation. Now, as to the criticism brought by Evangelicals, I think it has a lot of merit. Every system has strengths and weaknesses, and often they work in direct opposition to one another. One of Catholicism's strengths is its theological unity and liturgical precision. One weakness is that it is easy for Catholics to get so caught up in all the ritual that they slack off on fellowship and discipleship. Many Evangelicals are adult converts; they became Evangelical in a very personal, usually powerful way and they carry that with them into their faith life. This is why they go to church even though there is no "pain of sin" if they skip out. This means that the average Evangelical church is likely to have many more fervent believers. That's a strength. The weakness is that the more "lukewarm" believers have little motivation to go or to grow. A related weakness caused by this is that Evangelical churches have to make their services attractive to people who are not necessarily very faithful, and that affects the experience of the faithful. So it's a tradeoff either way. Finally, there is also a difference of opinion on what constitutes growth in holiness. Many things that Catholics value are not seen as spiritually advantageous by Evangelicals and vice versa. So we need to be careful which criteria of judgment we apply.

Similarly, you indicate that Evangelicals lack a legitimate authority and thus ultimately rely on private judgment, with predictably widely disparate views emerging on any number of theological issues. But Catholics also seem to hold widely disparate theological views—the typical Evangelical view of a monolithic Catholic experience tends to caricature. How is Catholicism different on this point?

This comes up often in discussions of religious authority and unity. It is important for non-Catholics to understand that the Church is not a theological democracy—we don't define doctrines by majority rule. The Church's dogma is settled and beyond anyone in the Church to change it. Thus, it is very unlike Evangelicalism, where any given group just is the sum total of its members (who typically come together based on their theological agreement). In that situation, disagreement can take hold and change the nature of a given group. The only choice at that point is to split the group up into various belief segments (hence its "multiplication by division" history). The Catholic Church's unity is found in its historic, authoritative, apostolic leadership, so the disagreement of any number of its members does not threaten its unity, because to the degree that Catholics disagree with the Church's dogma, to that degree they are not in communion with the Church anymore.

That seems a bit abstract, perhaps. One hears, for instance, of de facto schism in the Church; namely, that Church unity exists on paper but not in reality. Again, many of my own friends ask me this question: Is Church unity real, or is it simply a statement on paper, especially in an age like our own when so many Catholics dissent?

I would say it is a very real quality that is nonetheless difficult to quantify. The Church's definition of unity is rather straightforward, but identification of who partakes of that unity poses problems. A significant source of the difficulty is that a given person can be legitimately categorized as a Catholic even if they are in complete disagreement with the Catholic Church. This is because one does not become Catholic simply by agreeing with Church dogma, but rather by baptism. Because baptism is indelible on the Catholic account, dissent does not change the person's identification as Catholic. However, membership in most non-Catholic Christian groups is almost solely predicated on one's agreement with a given set of doctrinal affirmations. Consequently, disagreement with a group's doctrine automatically removes them from that group. So to call someone a Calvinist who denies the doctrines of total depravity and perseverance of the saints would simply make no sense. However, calling someone a Catholic who affirms abortion and denies Christ's resurrection does make sense, but in a different way. I think this paradigmatic difference gives the appearance of strength to claims that are true in a sense but really cannot do the work they are meant to do in an argument.

What would you most want a Catholic to understand about Evangelicalism?

I think there are two errors to avoid. The first is to see Evangelicals as superficial simply because their religious culture often lacks the depth of Catholicism. There are many Evangelicals who long for authenticity in their worship but who simply cannot find it in the current "ecclesial consumerist" culture much of the movement finds itself in today. The second is to see Evangelicalism as just a harmless non-Catholic movement that is essentially compatible with Catholicism. Although most Evangelicals don't know enough about Catholicism to warrant strong prejudice, they are often implicitly taught that it is a corrupt system peddling a false gospel (many ex-Catholic Evangelicals say they never heard the true gospel until they came to an Evangelical church).

What would you most want an Evangelical to understand about Catholicism?

I'd want them to see that they probably do not really understand what Catholicism is, and that their knee-jerk reactions are likely more emotional than rational. It takes quite a bit of study and interaction to really grasp the essential similarities and differences between the two groups—even down to the words used to express each group's views. Easy answers in this sad conflict are often false for both sides.

Several examples come to mind. Catholics use the word *evangelize* to refer to practically every aspect of Church life that aids in one's spiritual growth, whereas Protestants typically narrow the meaning down to preaching basic elements of the gospel. Protestants, following Martin Luther, typically see most if not all references to "works" in the Bible as being what St. Paul actually calls "works of the law" which are a subcategory of works having to do with Jewish rituals and not simply good works as such. Because Catholics follow St. Paul and not Luther, Protestants often equate what they say about doing good works with Legalism. Or take the Catholic notion of merit. In Latin, merit does not simply mean "earn"; it has several nuanced definitions. What Protestants often think when they hear the word *merit* is equivalent to *wages*, but the Catholic notion of merit is more like a tip. In a sense, both a wage and a tip are "earned," but they are earned on radically different terms. So for ecumenical dialogue to be fruitful, many longstanding misunderstandings need to be cleared away first.

Notes on Contributors

Sister Mary Prudence Allen, RSM, is a philosopher and member of the Religious Sisters of Mercy of Alma, Michigan. She received her PhD in philosophy from Claremont Graduate School of California in 1967 and then taught Philosophy at Concordia University for the next thirty years. In 2014, Pope Francis included Sister Prudence among the thirty theologians and philosophers he named to the International Theological Commission. In 2015, she returned to the United States and is presently an independent scholar lecturing and publishing and has just been assigned to help open a new convent for the Sisters of Mercy in Toledo, Ohio.

Hadley Arkes joined the faculty of Amherst College in 1966, and has been the Edward Ney Professor of Jurisprudence since 1987, assuming *emeritus* status in 2016. His many books include *The Philosopher in the City, First Things, Beyond the Constitution, Natural Rights and the Right to Choose*, and *Constitutional Illusions and Anchoring Truths: The Touchstone of the Natural Law*. His articles have appeared in professional journals and in the *Wall Street Journal, Weekly Standard*, and *National Review*. He has been a contributor to *First Things*, a journal that took its name from his book of that title.

He was the main architect of the bill that became known as the Born-Alive Infants' Protection Act. The account of his experience is contained as an epilogue to *Natural Rights & the Right to Choose*. Arkes first prepared his proposal as part of the debating kit assembled for the first George Bush in 1988. Later, he led the testimony on the bill before the Judiciary Committee of the US House, passing in both the House and Senate in 2002. The second President Bush signed the bill into law with Professor Arkes in attendance.

At Amherst, he founded the Committee for the American Founding, a group of alumni and students seeking to preserve the doctrines of "natural rights" taught by the American Founders and Lincoln, and also a new center for jurisprudence, in Washington, DC, the James Wilson Institute on Natural Rights and the American Founding.

Erika Bachiochi is a legal scholar at the Ethics and Public Policy Center specializing in Equal Protection jurisprudence, feminist legal theory, Catholic social teaching, and sexual ethics. She is also a Visiting Scholar at Harvard Law School and a Research Fellow at the Abigail Adams Institute in Cambridge, MA.

Her essays have appeared in publications such as the *Harvard Journal of Law and Public Policy*, *Christian Bioethics* (Oxford University), *First Things*, CNN.com, *National Review Online*, *Claremont Review of Books*, SCOTUSblog, and *Public Discourse*. She is the editor of two books, *Women, Sex & the Church: A Case for Catholic Teaching* (Pauline Books & Media, 2010) and *The Cost of "Choice": Women Evaluate the Impact of Abortion* (Encounter Books, 2004). She is a contributor to the Law Professor Blogs Network blog *Mirror of Justice* and serves on the Advisory Council of the Catholic Women's Forum and the Advisory Board of the Susan B. Anthony Birthplace Museum. She co-founded St. Benedict's, a classical Catholic school in Massachusetts where she served as President of the Board from 2013–2015.

Ms. Bachiochi received her BA from Middlebury

College, her MA in Theology as a Bradley Fellow at the Institute for the Study of Politics and Religion at Boston College, and her law degree from Boston University School of Law. She is currently working on a book on women's rights.

Douglas M. Beaumont has a PhD in theology from North-West University and an MA in apologetics from Southern Evangelical Seminary, where he served as assistant to President Norman Geisler and taught Bible and religion for many years. He is the author of *Evangelical Exodus: Evangelical Seminarians and Their Paths to Rome, The Message Behind the Movie,* and has contributed to *The Best Catholic Writing, The Apologetics Study Bible for Students,* and the *Christian Apologetics Journal.* He lives in California with his wife and four children.

Lucy Beckett studied history at Cambridge and is the author of several works of fiction, including *The Leaves are Falling, A Postcard from the Volcano,* and *The Time Before You Die: A Novel of the Reformation,* as well and her highly acclaimed work *In the Light of Christ: Writings in the Western Tradition.* She lives in Yorkshire, England, where she taught at Ampleforth Abbey.

Joshua Charles is an historian, writer, and speaker. He has authored and co-authored bestselling books on America's Founders, Israel, and the Bible. A concert pianist with an MA in government and a law degree, Joshua has performed and spoken around the world. His writing has been featured in numerous publications, including *Fox News, The Federalist,* and the *Jerusalem Post,* among others. He has served several organizations, including the Museum of the Bible, the American Bible Society, and the Jerusalem Institute of

Justice. After a lifetime spent as a born and raised Protestant, Joshua decided to become Catholic after spending nearly a year reading the Church Fathers, and more than 260 other books on the Catholic faith.

Cason Cheely is an attorney at Stone Crosby, PC. She resides with her husband, Dan, and their six children in the Philadelphia area where she serves on the Pastoral Council of the Archdiocese of Philadelphia and is involved with the CanaVox movement and Regina Angelorum Academy, a Catholic classical school. She received her JD *cum laude* from Notre Dame Law School in 2006 and her AB in the Woodrow Wilson School of Public and International Affairs at Princeton University in 2003. She studied Natural Law and Natural Rights with Professor Hadley Arkes at Princeton University during his tenure as a visiting fellow in the 2002–2003 academic year, and Professor Arkes advised her senior thesis entitled "Unto the Least of These: A Policy Framework for Embryo Adoption in the United States." She authored the chapter "Embryo Adoption and the Law" in *The Ethics of Embryo Adoption and the Catholic Tradition* (Brakman and Weaver, Springer: 2007).

Bishop James D. Conley was ordained a priest in 1985, serving as a parish priest in the Diocese of Wichita before earning his licentiate in Rome, where he later returned to serve as an official in the Vatican Congregation for Bishops. In 2001, Pope John Paul II named him "chaplain to his holiness" with the title of Monsignor. In 2008, Pope Benedict XVI appointed him as auxiliary bishop for the Archdiocese of Denver, with Denver Archbishop Charles J. Chaput ordaining him. Later, he would serve as apostolic administrator of the Denver Archdiocese, until Pope Benedict appointed him as the bishop of the Lincoln Diocese in

Nebraska. Bishop Conley was installed as the ninth bishop of Lincoln on November 20, 2012 in the Cathedral of the Risen Christ in Lincoln. For his episcopal motto, Bishop Conley, a convert to the Catholic faith, chose the same motto as the great nineteenth-century English convert John Henry Cardinal Newman, "*cor ad cor loquitur*," which means "heart speaks to heart."

Christina Deardurff is Assistant Editor at the monthly print journal *Inside the Vatican*. She is an alumna of Thomas Aquinas College in Santa Paula, California, and the mother of ten.

Birgitta Ekman was born in India, where her parents served as missionaries. For many years she has worked with a foundation she started, IndianChildren, which provides education, food and health care to many hundreds of Indian children. She has written five illustrated children's books based on her memories of her childhood in India and with Ulf co-authored *The Great Discovery* (*Den Stora Upptäckten—Vår Väg till Katolska Kyrkan*) about their journey to Rome.

Ulf Ekman was born in Gothenburg, Sweden and ordained a Lutheran minister in 1979, first serving as a university chaplain in Uppsala. In 1983 he founded Word of Life, a non-denominational Charismatic church in Uppsala, Sweden and was its Senior Pastor for thirty years. He founded several Bible schools and a seminary, has led conferences and seminars in many nations, including the former USSR, Eastern Europe, and India, and has written more than forty books & booklets, translated into over thirty languages. These include: *Take, Eat (A Book About the Holy Eucharist)*, *A Life of Worship*, *Jesus*, and *Our Holy Calling*.

Matthew J. Franck is Associate Director of the James Madison Program and Lecturer in Politics at Princeton University, Senior Fellow at the Witherspoon Institute, where he directs the Simon Center on Religion and the Constitution, and Professor Emeritus of Political|Science at Radford University, where he chaired the department and taught courses in political philosophy, constitutional law, and American politics. He has written, edited, or contributed to books published by the University Press of Kansas, Lexington Books, Oxford University Press, and Cambridge University Press, and has published articles and reviews in *American Political Thought*, the *Review of Politics*, the *Journal of Church and State*, the *Catholic Social Science Review*, *National Affairs*, *The New Atlantis*, *First Things*, the *Weekly Standard*, the *Claremont Review of Books*, *National Review*, and *Public Discourse*.

Timothy Fuller, born in Chicago in 1940, is a professor of political theory at Colorado College, a liberal arts college in Colorado Springs, where he has taught since 1965. In a career of wide-ranging teaching and scholarship in political philosophy, Fuller has focused most of all on the work of English thinkers from Thomas Hobbes to Michael Oakeshott.

Robert P. George holds Princeton's celebrated McCormick Chair in Jurisprudence and is the Director of the James Madison Program in American Ideals and Institutions. He has served as chairman of the United States Commission on International Religious Freedom, and before that on the President's Council on Bioethics and as a presidential appointee to the United States Commission on Civil Rights. He has also served as the US member of UNESCO's World Commission on the Ethics of Scientific

Knowledge and Technology. His many books include *In Defense of Natural Law, Making Men Moral; Embryo: A Defense of Human Life,* and *What is Marriage? Man and Woman: A Defense.* A graduate of Swarthmore College, he holds JD and MTS degrees from Harvard University and the degrees of DPhil, BCL, and DCL from Oxford University.

Gabrielle Girgis is a PhD student in politics at Princeton University. Motivated by a general interest in the fields of political theory, moral philosophy, and religion, her dissertation explores the nature and political-philosophical grounds of religious liberty. Specifically, it investigates the proper basis and scope for this principle as a distinct right of legal protection for religion and conscience. Central to her project is an effort to explain the human and public value of religion and conscience, and to draw moral-legal implications from that account for civil liberties in a pluralist liberal democracy. Before pursuing her PhD at Princeton, she earned a BA in the Program of Liberal Studies from the University of Notre Dame.

Sherif Girgis, a PhD student in philosophy at Princeton and a Catholic convert from (lapsed) Coptic Orthodoxy, has written and spoken widely in academic and popular venues on moral, religious, and social issues. A 2008 graduate of Princeton, *summa cum laude*, he earned a JD from Yale and a BPhil (MPhil) in philosophy from Oxford as a Rhodes Scholar.

Hope Kean, a convert herself, graduated from Princeton University in 2018. She is a member of Princeton's Aquinas community and a student member of the Thomistic Institute, part of the Dominican House of Studies in Washington, DC.

Erika Kidd is Assistant Professor and Director of the Master of Arts in Catholic Studies at the University of St. Thomas in St. Paul, Minnesota. She did her undergraduate degree at Baylor University and graduate work in philosophy at Villanova. She writes on Augustine and the Augustinian tradition.

Kathryn Jean Lopez is senior editor at the National Review Institute where she directs the Center for Religion, Culture, and Civil Society and is editor-at-large of *National Review* magazine. She's been at *NR* for over twenty years and was previously editor of *NR*'s website. She's a nationally syndicated columnist and contributor to many publications including *Angelus* from the Archdiocese of Los Angeles and fortnightly columnist at *OSV Newsweekly*. She's been published by the *Wall Street Journal* and the *New York Times* and appeared on CNN and Fox News among others, including EWTN. She was awarded the annual Washington Women in Journalism Award for Outstanding Journalism in the Periodic Press from CQ *Roll Call* in 2016 for writing about Christian genocide and persecution. Lopez serves on a number of boards and is a member of the Pro-Life Commission of the Archdiocese of New York, and speaks frequently on "first principle" issues including virtue, especially gratitude. She's co-author of *How to Defend the Faith without Raising Your Voice* (OSV) and a contributor to *When Women Pray* (Sophia), among other books. In 2012, Pope Benedict XVI presented her with a message for women throughout the world, as a representative of all the women of the world. A graduate of the Catholic University of America, she's also a certified spiritual director through the Cenacle of Our Lady of Divine Providence School of

Spirituality and the Franciscan University of Steubenville, which focuses on Ignatius's approach to the spiritual life.

Karin Öberg is a Professor of Astronomy at Harvard University and leader of the Öberg Astrochemistry Group at the Harvard-Smithsonian Center for Astrophysics. Raised in Sweden, she received a Bachelor of Science degree at the California Institute of Technology and a PhD at Leiden University. She received a Hubble Postdoctoral Fellowship from NASA, is widely published, and serves on the board of the Society of Catholic Scientists.

Chad Pecknold received his PhD from the University of Cambridge (UK) and since 2008 he has been a Professor of Historical & Systematic Theology in the School of Theology at the Catholic University of America. He teaches in the areas of fundamental theology, Christian anthropology, and political theology. He is the author of a number scholarly articles and books including, most recently, *Christianity and Politics: A Brief Guide to the History* and *The T&T Clark Companion to Augustine and Modern Theology*. Pecknold is also a frequent contributor to debates in the public square, writing regular columns for *First Things* and *National Review* and has appeared as an invited guest on radio and television shows such as NPR's "All Things Considered," Vatican Radio, Al Jazeera America, BBC World News, ABC News, FOX News, CNBC Squawk Box, and he is a regular contributor on EWTN News Nightly offering his clear analysis and expert opinion on the Catholic Church, the papacy, and the relationship between the Church and politics in American culture.

Nathaniel Peters is the Executive Director of the Morningside Institute and a lecturer at Columbia University. He received a BA from Swarthmore College, an MTS from the University of Notre Dame, and the PhD from Boston College in the history of Christian thought and ethics. He has published articles and reviews in a variety of scholarly and popular venues.

Kirsten Powers is a columnist for *USA Today*, a CNN Political Analyst, and co-host of the podcast *The Faith Angle*. Previously a Fox News Channel commentator, she is author of *The Silencing* (Regnery). Powers wrote in 2013 about her conversion to Christianity in *Christianity Today* (which became their most read web story for the year) and contributed "The first Noel: Christmas with Jesus" to the book *The Christmas Virtues* (Templeton). A native of Alaska, she lives in Washington, DC.

Matthew Schmitz is senior editor of *First Things*. His writing has appeared in the *New York Times*, *Washington Post*, *Spectator*, and other publications. He holds an AB in English from Princeton University.

R. J. Snell directs the Center on the University and Intellectual Life at the Witherspoon Institute in Princeton, NJ. Prior to this appointment he was for many years Professor of Philosophy and Director of the Philosophy Program at Eastern University and the Templeton Honors College, where he founded and directed the Agora Institute for Civic Virtue and the Common Good. A convert to Catholicism, he grew up Baptist and received his early education at the schools of Prairie Bible Institute and Liberty University. His first encounter with Rome occurred while pursuing an MA in philosophy at Boston College, where he took several courses with Peter Kreeft. Later he earned a PhD in philosophy at Marquette University. He is the author of several books as well as articles, chapters, and essays in a variety of scholarly and popular venues. He and his family reside in the Princeton area.

Emily Sullivan is a graduate of the great books program of Thomas Aquinas College, California. She has taught high school philosophy and theology, worked as the Northeast Program Manager for Endow, and currently works for the Thomistic Institute based at the Dominican House of Studies, Washington, DC. She has spoken at Notre Dame, Princeton, and a variety of women's retreats and conferences on the thought of Sts. Thomas Aquinas, Edith Stein and John Paul II. She and her husband have three little girls and reside in the Archdiocese of Philadelphia where Emily serves on Archbishop Chaput's Pastoral Council.

Helena M. Tomko is assistant professor of literature in the Department of Humanities at Villanova University. She grew up in the Northeast of England, before completing her undergraduate degree in German and Italian at the University of Bristol and her DPhil in German at St. John's College, Oxford University. Her scholarship focuses on German Catholic literature and intellectual culture during the Weimar Republic and Third Reich, as well as on the sacramental vision in Catholic fiction.

Adrian Vermeule is the Ralph S. Tyler Professor of Constitutional Law at Harvard Law School. A graduate of Harvard College ('90) and Harvard Law School ('93), he served as a law clerk for the late Justice Antonin Scalia in 1994–95, and has authored or co-authored eight books, including *Law's Abnegation: From Law's Empire to the Administrative State*.

Michael Ward is Senior Research Fellow at Blackfriars Hall, University of Oxford. He is the author of the award-winning *Planet Narnia: The Seven Heavens in the Imagination of C. S. Lewis* and co-editor of *The Cambridge Companion to C. S. Lewis* and *C. S. Lewis at Poets' Corner*. Ward presented the BBC1 television documentary *The Narnia Code* (2009), directed and produced by the BAFTA-winning film-maker Norman Stone, and authored an accompanying book entitled *The Narnia Code: C. S. Lewis and the Secret of the Seven Heavens*.

Previously, Dr. Ward served as Chaplain of St. Peter's College in the University of Oxford and Chaplain of Peterhouse in the University of Cambridge. He was resident Warden of The Kilns, Lewis's Oxford home, from 1996 to 1999.

Thomas Joseph White, OP, entered the Order of Preachers in 2003. His research and teaching have focused particularly on topics related to Thomistic metaphysics and Christology as well as Roman Catholic-Reformed ecumenical dialogue. He is the author of *Wisdom in the Face of Modernity: A Study in Thomistic Natural Theology*, *The Incarnate Lord: A Thomistic Study in Christology*, and *The Light of Christ: An Introduction to Catholicism*. In 2011 he was appointed an ordinary member of the Pontifical Academy of St. Thomas Aquinas.

Julia Yost is senior editor of *First Things*. She is a PhD candidate in English at Yale University and holds an MFA in fiction from Washington University in St. Louis.